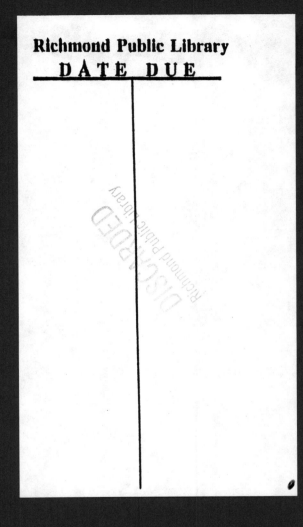

STUKA
Ju-87

STUKA
Ju-87

Lt-Col A. J. Barker

CHARTWELL BOOKS INC.

A Bison Book

First published in the USA by
Chartwell Books Inc.
A Division of Books Sales Inc.
110 Enterprise Avenue
Secaucus, New Jersey 07094

Copyright © 1980 Bison Books Limited

Produced by
Bison Books Limited
4 Cromwell Place
London SW7

ISBN: 0-89009-323-7
Library of Congress Catalog Card Number 79-57097

Printed in Hong Kong

Page 1: The early exhaust identifies this as a B-1. It presents an almost perfect plan view for the camera and in so doing shows the dive brakes, wing racks, closely spatted wheels and tail-plane bracing struts which are not often so visible in conventional views.
Page 2-3: Three Ju87B-2s pose for the camera in an early war-publicity picture.
Page 4-5: This Ju87B-2 is identified as a machine of StG2 by the T6 marking forward of the cross. The E after the cross is the individual letter, and the M indicates that it is a 4th Staffel aircraft. The 4th Staffel would be part of II Gruppe, so the unit designation could be written II/StG 2.

CONTENTS

THE STUKA CONCEPT

None of the aircraft of World War II have enjoyed as much notoriety as the controversial evil-looking German Ju87 – better known as the 'Stuka' (an abbreviation of *Sturz-kampfflugzeug*, a word which describes all dive bombers). It was, as its German name suggests, a bomber which delivered its lethal cargo during a steep dive toward the target. The pilot aimed the plane; he had no need of the complicated sighting devices used in the conventional straight-and-level bombers. It was a remarkably accurate and versatile method of bombing and for men at the target end of an attack the sight and sound of a flight of dive bombers screaming down from a height of 10,000ft or so was a frightening experience.

The Stuka concept has been attributed to Ernst Udet, a gregarious and ebullient air ace who had become a stunt flier after World War I. Udet travelled widely and was popular wherever he went, especially in America. In 1931 he attended an international air rally in Cleveland, Ohio, in the United States and it was here that he got the idea. During the rally a Curtiss Hawk fighter-bomber was put through its paces, and Udet was fascinated as he watched its pilot diving almost vertically to drop sacks of sand onto a tiny circle representing an enemy target. This kind of stunt would clearly appeal to audiences attending the sort of show put on by Udet's air circus, and Udet decided he must have one of these planes. However, a Hawk cost about 60,000 Reichsmark (US $15,000), a sum which was way beyond the flier's means at that time. However Udet had many friends, among them Hermann Göring, a wartime comrade and fellow pilot in the famous Richthofen squadron. Göring, quick to appreciate the military potential of aircraft like the Hawk, offered to advance the money. So a Curtiss Hawk was bought and shipped in November 1933 to Bremerhaven, where the customs formalities usually attending the import of a foreign warplane were swept aside by the German Air Ministry. One month later it was flown by Udet at an official demonstration in Berlin and a crash program to produce a German *Sturzbomber* was authorized shortly afterward.

Others in Germany and elsewhere had also been thinking of a fighter-bomber capable of diving steeply and carrying a bomb of at least 250kg of explosive. By diving such an aircraft onto the target and releasing the bomb just before the pilot levelled off and turned away, it was reasoned, the bomb would be more accurately placed. Furthermore since 1928 a team of German engineers led by Hermann Pohlmann had been working secretly in Sweden on the techniques of dive bombing. They used an old single-seater Junkers biplane flown by a World War I veteran fighter pilot, Captain Willy Neuenhofen. Dives at angles of 60–80 degrees from the vertical were tried out and dummy bombs were released at about 800m above the ground while the aircraft was still in a dive. The results were distinctly promising, since the bomb invariably fell on or very close to the target – a consistent accuracy never previously attained with straight-and-level bombing methods. It was clear that the accuracy would have been even better had it not been that the plane tended to yaw in the diving position.

Most of Neuenhofen's test flights were made in the winter months, and flying a machine with a open cockpit in a Swedish winter was an uncomfortable business in itself. Other hazards stemmed from the need to use a frozen lake in lieu of a proper airfield and in the early days of the test flight program, to fly at night. Secrecy was not the reason for the latter. The experimental dives were filmed for subsequent analysis by coupling a camera to a theodolite. A searchlight was fitted to the belly of the aircraft and flares to the practice bombs. The plane dived with its searchlight on but when the bomb was released the searchlight was automatically dowsed and the path of the falling bomb was indicated by the flare. Fortunately for Neuenhofen, techniques were developed to make daytime flights possible. Cameras were mounted on the aircraft, one pointing downward to the bomb, another above the pilot's head photographing the instrument readings in the cockpit.

Back in Germany work had already started on the development of a conventional single-seater fighter, the Henschel 123, before Udet stimulated Göring's interest in the *Sturzbomber*. When this trim and relatively unsophisticated biplane rolled off the production lines it was to be issued to the Luftwaffe. Although the Henschel was intended to be employed primarily as a fighter, the possibility of it being used to give close support to ground troops by strafing and bombing was now considered. Thus it was that in April 1934 orders were issued for one of the Luftwaffe's recently formed fighter squadrons equipped with Henschels to practice dive bombing techniques. This squadron was to be expanded into a Stuka Wing – the *Gruppe Schwerin*, subsequently redesignated in April 1935 the *Immelmann Gruppe* – and the intention was that it would eventually be equipped with a more advanced plane capable of a near vertical dive.

The specification for the new plane was issued by the *Technisches Amt* of the German Air Ministry in January 1935 and three aircraft manufacturers, Arado, Heinkel, and Junkers, were each charged with constructing a prototype. Within three months the first prototype, Ju87V-1, was undergoing test flights at Dessau.

This first machine, like its successors, was an ugly looking aircraft resembling in appearance a predatory bird with extended talons. But the Ju87 was to prove a very rugged airplane, with relatively high maneuverability. In this prototype the engine was a supercharged 12-cylinder liquid-cooled Rolls-Royce Kestrel, developing 525hp for takeoff and driving a two-bladed fixed-pitch wooden airscrew. During the test flights at Dessau, however, it was found that the Kestrel engine tended to overheat and an enlarged radiator bath had to be fitted. This made the machine look even uglier than before and contributed to the predatory bird impression, since in flight the radiator bath looked like a gaping beak.

Air brakes were to have been fitted under the wings of the prototype but these were not ready when the first test dives were attempted during the summer of 1935. This resulted in a nasty accident, for when the pilot tried to level out during a medium-angle dive the entire tail assembly broke off from the fuselage and the aircraft crashed. Meanwhile the second prototype, the Ju87V-2, powered by a Junkers Jumo V-12 engine rated at 610hp driving a three-bladed variable pitch airscrew, was almost ready to be put through its paces. However the test flying of this machine was delayed until the experts investigating the cause of the crash of the first had completed their work. Their findings led to a complete redesign of the tail assembly.

By the time the test program was resumed in the autumn of 1935, the third prototype, the Ju87V-3, was also ready to take to the air. Both it and the Ju87V-2 had been fitted with dive brakes and in March 1936 the two machines participated in comparative trials with the Heinkel He 118, the Arado Ar 81 and the Hamburger Flugzeugbau's Ha 137. At these trials the Ju87 was judged to be superior, and best fitted for issue to the *Stukagruppen* that were now planned. To some of the German aircraft designers and aviators it seemed that the adoption of the Ju87 had been a foregone conclusion anyway, and although the dive-bombing concept had many adherents in the Luftwaffe it also had some resolute opponents. Foremost among the latter was Oberst Baron Wolfram von Richthofen, chief of the Development Section of the Luftwaffe's *Technisches Amt*, who on 9 June 1936 issued a confidential directive ordering development of the Ju87 to be halted. On the following day, however, Göring put Ernst Udet in charge of the *Technisches Amt* and the latter immediately rescinded his predecessor's directive. The stage was now set for mass production of the Ju87 and the first of the new dive bombers, known as the Ju87A-1, came off the assembly line toward the end of 1936.

Meanwhile Göring's ideas and ambitions were expanding

Above: Ernst Udet was head of the Luftwaffe's Technisches Amt, which developed the Ju87.
Below: The biplane Henschel 123 was used by the Luftwaffe to test their theories on dive bombing. It was used in this role and as a ground-support aircraft as late as 1944. This aircraft is in prewar splinter camouflage and has its fin swastika on a red band. It is an early A-1 version serving with II/StG165 Immelmann.

Above: This Henschel Hs 123A-1 was photographed in Russia in early 1942 when it was serving with 8/SG1. The marking forward of the fuselage cross is a black triangle signifying a *Schlachtgruppe* aircraft. It is fitted with bomb racks beneath the wings and fuselage. The band around the rear fuselage is a yellow tactical marking.

Below: This is the twelfth production Ju87A-1 and carries the civil registration D-IEAU although it is camouflaged in early Luftwaffe three-tone splinter. The small 12 above the tailplane support is its production number. Of interest is the early design gunner's canopy with a slot through which the rear defensive machine gun was fired.

and he was now thinking in terms of six *Stukagruppen* of which four were to be equipped with the Ju87. These were I and II/St G162 (redesignated later St G 123 and subsequently StG2), I/StG262 (redesignated later I/StG2) and III/StG165 (redesignated later III/StG51). Each group was to have 39 planes – three squadrons of twelve, and three other aircraft for the wing commander and his staff – this was to give a first-line *Gruppe* strength of 156 Stukas.

Between 1936 and 1939 the Spanish Civil War gave Göring an opportunity to try out his new aircraft with the Condor Legion, and a number of Luftwaffe officers gained valuable operational experience in action over Spain. Foremost among these were Wolfram von Richthofen (the former chief of the Development Section of the Luftwaffe's *Technisches Amt* and opponent of the dive-bomber concept) and the dark and dashing fighter pilot, Adolf Galland. As an *Oberleutnant*, Galland flew more than 300 sorties over Spain between 1937 and 1938, mostly in Heinkel He-51s and Messerschmitt 109s.

The role of the Condor Legion was close support of the infantry and the brunt was borne initially by the fighters and fighter-bombers flown by men like Galland. Toward the end of 1937 however a *Kette* (Flight) of three Ju87As from the first Stuka Wing, the *Immelmann Gruppe*, was sent to Spain to try out dive-bombing techniques. The first operation involving this trio of Stukas was at Teruel and they subsequently saw action on the Ebro and Catalonian fronts. In order to give as many pilots as possible experience in operational conditions, officers of the Gruppe were rotated with the *Kette* in Spain. In an era when radio communications was in its infancy and flight tactics were directed by hand signals, many lessons were learned. For the dive-bomber pilots one of the most impor-

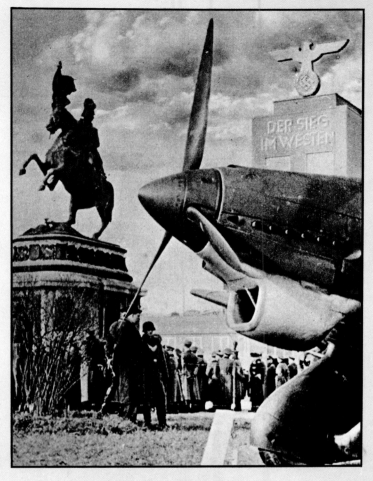

Above: The prototypes and early A versions of the Ju87 had a clean cowling line to their Jumo 210Ca twelve-cylinder engines. They were also fitted with a trousered undercarriage fairing which was far more prominent than the later 'spats.' These features are clearly visible on this aircraft which stands before the monument to Archduke Charles, the hero of Aspern.

tant factors was that pilots could blackout and lose control when they pulled out of their dive. (On one occasion a whole formation of Ju87s in Spain was late in pulling out and many hit the ground.) The effects of the centrifugal forces which came into play when a pilot pulled out of a steep dive were not fully understood at this time. Nor was it easy to pull the earlier planes out of their dives. Later versions of the Stuka embodied a number of refinements which eased the pilot's task. Those who flew a Ju87A-1 or a Ju87A-2 had to remember to complete a complicated sequence of functions before and during a dive – throttling back, closing the cooling gills, switching over to a sea-level supercharger and turning the airscrew to coarse pitch before and during the dive – and reversing the process after pulling out.

The Ju87A-2 went into production at Dessau toward the end of 1937 and by the early summer of 1938 some 200 of the A-series Stukas had been delivered to the Luftwaffe. Late in 1937 it was decided to phase out the A planes and to produce a redesigned Stuka, fitted with a more powerful engine. Designated the Ju87B, the first of the new machines were

Left: Comparison of the nose of this early production B-1 version with that of the A shown on page 9 (top) shows how the closely-cowled Jumo engine has now developed a much larger chin radiator and air intake for oil cooling behind the enormous propeller.

delivered to the Luftwaffe in the autumn of 1938. Production meantime had been transferred from the Junkers Dessau factory to the Berlin-Tempelhof plant of the 'Weser' Flugzeugbau. The Jumo 211 engine which powered the Ju87B was almost twice as powerful as the Jumo 210 of the Ju87A and the aircraft itself was fitted with an automatic device – almost an autopilot – to ensure a proper pull-out from a steep dive. The wings and tail assembly of the Ju87B were very similar to those of its predecessor, but the trousered landing gear of the Ju87A was replaced by cantilever units with streamlined spats and the shape of the fuselage was slightly different. But the most important difference made by the new engine was that a 500kg bomb could be carried as well as the crew of two. (The Ju87A could also carry a 500kg bomb, but only if the plane was flown as a single seater.)

Five of the new Ju87Bs (subsequently known as Ju87B-1s) were sent to Spain in October 1938 where they emulated the successes of the *Kette* of Ju87As that had preceded them. Meantime production at the Berlin-Tempelhof plant was stepped up and by mid-1939 more than sixty Ju87Bs were coming off the production line. In consequence by 1 September 1939 all of the Luftwaffe's nine *Stukagruppen* had been equipped with the Ju87B-1. (The Ju87As with which they had previously been equipped were withdrawn and turned over to training units.) Thus at the beginning of World War II the Stuka Wings possessed 336 Ju87Bs; 288 were serviceable.

Right: Adolf Galland flew with the Condor Legion in Spain.
Below: This side view of a Ju87B-1 presents the aircraft's profile to advantage. Rear defensive armament is a 7.92mm **MG15** and the barrel of one of the two wing-mounted 7.92mm **MG17s** can be seen just above the wheel spat. The marking in the top left-hand segment of the fuselage cross is a location point for first-aid equipment.

ROLE, TACTICS AND TE

At the outbreak of World War II the Luftwaffe was probably the strongest air force in the world. It was a tactical force, mainly developed to co-operate closely with the army on the ground – a role ideally suited to the Stuka. Nevertheless some senior Luftwaffe officers considered that the Stuka was obsolescent because of its relatively low speed and vulnerability, and production was scheduled to cease by the end of 1939. However, the Stuka's successful performance in Poland brought a change of heart and Göring ordered that production of the Ju87 should not only continue but actually be stepped up. As a result 611 Stukas were delivered to the Luftwaffe during 1940.

Both in Poland and subsequently in France and the Low Countries the dive bomber was an essential component of the *blitz* technique. If German artillery could not dominate the battlefield, German aircraft generally could. And so began the legend of the Stuka. Without this aircraft Hitler's armored

columns would never have been able to make such rapid advances in the first two and a half years of the war. However one shortcoming of the Ju87 soon became apparent. All too often its relatively short range (600km) restricted its employment in close support of mechanized columns slicing deep into enemy territory. At the beginning of a campaign this was not a problem but as the panzers advanced, the Stukas, operating from their same airfields, were able to spend progressively less time over the battlefield. Ultimately, of course, they had either to find or build new airfields closer to the front. In underdeveloped countries like the USSR very few airfields existed, and neither the Luftwaffe nor the German Army's sappers had developed the skills or the equipment necessary for the quick construction of emergency airstrips. In countries such as France where airfields did exist the problem was more usually the hazards associated with the appearance of enemy aircraft while the Stukas were taking off or landing.

Below: **This Ju87B-2 is being operated by the 2nd Staffel of StG1 over France in 1940. The unit also operated with success in Poland but the single 7.92mm MG15, seen in the rear cockpit, afforded little protection against RAF fighters when the unit took part in the campaigns in France and England in the summer of 1940.**

CHNIQUES

Above: These Ju87B-2s are flying in the classic 'finger four' formation which was first used by the Luftwaffe and later copied by practically every air force. By spreading the fingers of the hand it is possible to see how the name was derived. The fifth aircraft (nearest the camera) has in fact made this more of a 'finger five' formation.
Above right: These aircraft are Ju87Bs of StG3 operating over the Gobi desert. The sight of the approach of such a force must have been somewhat demoralizing to beleagured infantrymen.

Right: This heavily retouched publicity photograph clearly shows the underwing dive brakes and bomb racks of what was originally captioned as a B-1. It is likely that most of this particular aircraft is drawn from imagination.

Below: This sequence illustrates the release of the center-line bomb from its cradle. The aircraft is aimed at the target and just prior to reaching the release point the cradle is swung out to take the bomb clear of the propeller arc. In the last frame it can be seen falling clear of the aircraft.

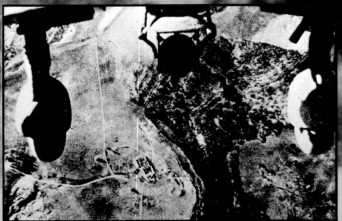

The effect of the dive brake

Without dive brake

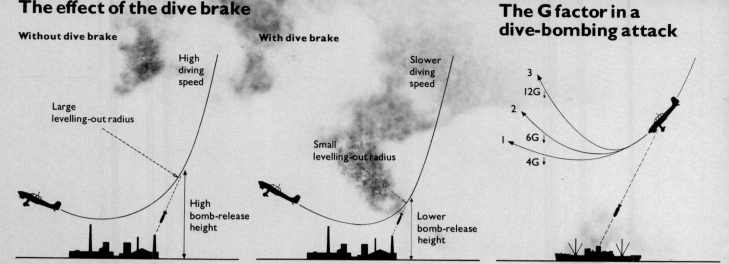

High
diving
speed

Large
levelling-out radius

High
bomb-release
height

Less accuracy

With dive brake

Slower
diving
speed

Small
levelling-out radius

Lower
bomb-release
height

Greater accuracy

The G factor in a dive-bombing attack

3
12G

2
6G

1
4G

Above: One of the attractions of the dive bomber was that the whole aircraft was aimed at the target, thus making accuracy of bombing much easier to attain.

Without using the aircraft's dive brakes a steep angle of dive resulted in a high descent requiring more air space in which to recover. In this condition it was necessary for the pilot to initiate dive recovery much sooner and bombing accuracy suffered as a result.

When the dive brakes were used they checked the aircraft's diving speed, thus enabling a lower level to be reached before the dive was terminated. This led to greater accuracy, a slower recovery, a less shallow recovery radius and lower G forces on the crew.

When an aircraft pulls out of a dive both pilot and plane are subjected to a centrifugal force which varies according to the steepness of the curved path taken by the machine. The human body can withstand only so much of this stress, the effect of which is to make the body seem heavier. With a force of 1G for example, the body appears to be twice as heavy as normal. A force of 4G can be tolerated for four to five seconds – which proved to be ample time for a Stuka pilot to level off (see Curve 1). At 6G (Curve 2) Stuka pilots usually blacked out after five seconds and at 12G (Curve 3) they were unconscious within two seconds.

Operational Stuka Wings comprised two, three or four squadrons. Wings co-operating directly with armored formations operated independently, as did Wings whose squadrons had been specially trained for night-bombing operations; the rest were organized into Groups (Geschwader) each of three Wings. At full strength every squadron had sixteen Stukas and the Wing and Group headquarters personnel each had four more. When hostilities broke out in 1939 the standard Stuka armament was a couple of 7.92mm machine guns, one firing forward and the other in a flexible mounting in the rear cockpit. By mid-1943, however, these had been replaced by two 20mm forward-firing cannons under the wings, and twin machine guns in the rear cockpit. About this time a tank-busting Stuka, the Ju87G-1, also appeared. Soon after the German invasion of the USSR a whole Stuka Group attacked a concentration of about sixty Soviet tanks, fifty miles south of Grodno and later discovered that only one tank had been knocked out. The conclusion was that unless a tank received a direct hit bombs were inadequate, and so some Stukas (Ju 87D-5s) were converted to carry a pair of 37mm flak 18 cannons beneath the wings close to the undercarriage. The cannons fired armor-piercing ammunition and as they were detachable they could be replaced by bomb racks when the aircraft was not required in a tank-busting role. As the war drew to a close, 4kg hollow charge bombs were found to be more effective than the cannon.

Against 'hard' and fixed targets high explosive bombs of 50–500kg size were customarily used. For attacks against men and vehicles there were fragmentation bombs of 1–500kg – the smaller 1kg and 2kg size being dropped in containers. To increase the fragmentation effect special fuses known as Dinort sticks were screwed into the nose caps of the larger bombs. These sticks were literally just that, causing the bomb to detonate some 30cm above the ground.

Depending on the target there were three basic forms of attack: a near vertical nose dive (Sturzangriff) onto the target, from a height of 2–5000m at an angle of 60–90 degrees; an oblique or shallow dive (Schrägangriff) from a height of 700–1500m at an angle of 20–50 degrees, and a low-level attack (Tiefangriff) – when the approach was made at a low altitude, never more than 300m. After a shallow dive approach bombs were usually released in a 3–600m long 'carpet' and the Stuka's machine guns used to strafe the target area. For a low-level bombing attack delayed action fuses were fitted to the bombs. In all three forms of attack the bombs were dropped singly or in pairs when possible.

The sight and sound of a Stuka going into a dive was enough to send a cold chill down the spine of anyone under attack and, to enhance the demoralizing effect, sirens operated by wooden propellers spun by the slipstream were mounted on the undercarriage spats. The pitch and intensity of the noise emitted by these 'Jericho Trumpets,' as they were called, increased as the aircraft gathered speed in the dive. The resultant ear-splitting shriek not only terrified the enemy but also scared many Stuka crews in their early stages of training.

Major Friedrich Lang, one of the most experienced dive-bomber pilots of World War II, has written that the dive bomber was best suited to the attack of small important targets such as bridges, ships, trains, buildings and armored fighting vehicles. Bombing accuracy depended on the angle of descent of the bomb and this was determined by the aircraft's diving angle. In Lang's opinion the most efficient diving angle

was roughly 70 degrees from the horizontal. Lines painted at various angles on the cabin side panels which the pilot aligned with the horizon facilitated aiming.

The role of the Stuka vis-à-vis that of the conventional bomber was never clearly defined, but the tendency was to employ Stukas primarily in direct support of ground operations rather than on missions into areas remote from the fighting. Unlike conventional bombers, Stukas rarely operated singly. Attacks were normally carried out by complete Wings, as experience showed that an assault, in successive flights of three, by a total of thirty or more Stukas usually guaranteed the destruction of the target. Thirty planes was the average operational strength (as against the established strength of 52) in a Wing of three squadrons. For mutual self-support the Stukas almost always flew in a tight-packed V formation – Vs by flights (that is, Ketten of three planes) grouped into squadron Vs, which in turn formed a Wing V. This permitted the maximum benefit to be derived from the overlapping fields of fire of the Stuka's machine guns.

Before World War II the tactics of a Stuka attack stipulated an approach at an altitude of about 6000m. The enemy could not be sure of the Stuka's objective at this height so an element of surprise was retained until the actual attack was launched; at the same time the dangers from anti-aircraft fire were minimal. As the Stukas neared their target they could drop down to the altitude at which they were to commence the bombing dives, where possible they attacked against the wind and from out of the sun. On completion of the mission the return flight to base was made in open formation, making maximum use of the cover afforded by cloud and the terrain.

These tactics changed in 1939 when Stuka operations in Poland showed that a 6000m approach to the target was unnecessary. Moreover the need to use oxygen masks at this altitude made it positively undesirable. From these early operations individual Stuka pilots also concluded that their attacks went better when they did not use the cumbersome dive brakes with which their Ju87B-1s were fitted. Admittedly in a 70 degree dive the brakes brought the speed down from 650kph to 450kph and so made aiming easier. Apart from being a tedious business, slamming the brakes in and out upset the flight formation and made the pilots nervous at a time when they were supposed to be concentrating on aligning the aircraft with the target and releasing the bombs. Another factor militating against use of the dive brakes was an upsurge in Polish anti-aircraft activity, when all too often the approach to and flight from the target area demanded more, not less, speed. In the event it was concluded that aiming, accuracy and the height at which bombs were released were not adversely affected when the air brakes were not used. Also the longer levelling-out radius at the end of the dive path resulting from the higher speed could be decreased by the pilot levelling out more sharply. The only snag about this was that doing so resulted in blood draining from the retina of the pilot's eyes producing a temporary loss of vision for about a second.

Mention has been made of the fitting of a device, the Höhenlader to the Ju87B version. This device cut in automatically during a dive, to relieve the pilot of the problem of when to level out. In theory the Höhenlader was a sensible and useful modification but in practice it was of dubious value because it interfered with the aiming process. For this reason the Höhenlader was not fitted to later versions of the Stuka, and the point at which the pilot pulled out of a dive was left to his discretion.

During the Polish campaign the Stukas were able to carry out their mission without any real concern for enemy fighter

Left: **This Ju87B-1 has released its five bombs in one salvo, the four small bombs have fallen from the wing racks, and the large one from the center-line cradle.**

Above: Dive bombers could only operate with impunity when total air superiority was achieved. In raids on England, and later in Russia, fighter escort was essential. This was often provided by the ubiquitous Bf 109, a G version of which shows off its underside to the camera aircraft on the Eastern Front.

aircraft, as the Polish Air Force rarely appeared. It was a different story when Germany invaded Russia however, and the need for German fighter cover soon became apparent. On their own the slow-flying Stukas could only hope to partially compensate for their vulnerability by maneuverability and by flying in formation. The immediate answer was for them to operate under the protection of German fighter aircraft. But this proved to be a short-term solution. During the second half of the campaign in North Africa, subsequently in Italy and later in northwest Europe, Allied air superiority coupled with a deterioration in the quality of air crew training virtually ruled out the employment of Stukas except in suicide missions. Therefore in the spring of 1944 most of the *Stukagruppen* started to convert to the Focke-Wulf FW190 and by the autumn of that year only one Ju87 group was still undertaking daylight sorties (this was Rudel's III/StG2 Wing on the Russian front).

Air-to-air and air-to-ground radio communication in Stuka units was strictly limited to that necessary for target location and recognition. Command of the Stuka wings was exercised by the Stuka Group HQ or – in the case of wings operating directly with army formations – by the division HQ concerned. In the latter case the appropriate Luftwaffe HQ had overriding control over matters associated with flying.

Orders for a mission would normally be issued to squadron commanders at a verbal briefing. At this conference 1:1,000,000, 1:300,000 or 1:100,000 scale maps, and air photographs if they were available, would be studied. Written orders were exceptional, and generally confined to broad directives usually issued at the beginning of a campaign. According to the situation at the front, squadrons would be standing by at a specific stage of readiness designated by a time requirement, for instance, 'Two hours.' 'Immediate' readiness meant that the aircraft, fuelled, serviced and bombed up, would be ready to take off literally at a moment's notice. The planes would be positioned near the airstrip, their crews would be close by, while the respective squadron and Wing commanders awaited orders in the Wing's tactical headquarters. At the briefing the targets to be attacked would be detailed, and the squadron commanders would be told how to recognize them and what to expect during the approach flight. They would also be told the sequence in which the various squadrons would fly, and be given orders

covering the height of approach, the method and direction of attack, the number of sorties to be made and how the Wing would fly back when the mission had been completed. The time of takeoff, the expected times of arrival in the target area and, if fighter cover was to be provided, the time and rendezvous with the fighter planes would be laid down. The state of enemy anti-aircraft defenses and atmospheric conditions would also be discussed.

After the briefing squadron commanders would brief their crews and go over the finer points of the forthcoming operation. Most of their problems were associated with keeping their planes in formation, locating the target and concentrating on it. When fighter cover was provided it was the responsibility of the fighter aircraft to take up a position best suited to the protection of the Stukas during the flight to the target area. If the formation was attacked by enemy aircraft *en route*, it was the job of the German fighters to deal with them. Under attack – with or without fighter cover – the Stukas tried to maintain their formation. On occasion, however, it was expedient to break away in order to concentrate the Stuka's own machine gun against the attackers. In the earlier days this revealed a snag because the Ju87 tail unit was in the field of fire when the gun mounted in the rear cockpit was traversed. (The problem was overcome eventually by fitting a bullet repeller to the tail.)

If the mission was in support of a ground action and the target was to be indicated by the troops below, the Wing commander would establish radio contact with the air liaison officer accompanying the troops about five minutes before the attack began. Gridded maps annotated by letters proved to be a quick and reliable means of relaying the information from ground to air. Once the target had been recognized and sighted, the squadron would shake out into an appropriate formation for the attack. Depending on the nature of the target this could vary from a single 'line-ahead' to a formation in which the squadrons flew in Vs abreast of each other. The V formation had the advantage that dropping the bombs was quicker and the Wing was better able to defend itself if enemy fighters pounced as the Stukas were leaving the target area. The only difficulty was that a closely packed formation restricted the maneuverability of individual planes and thus when they were taking evasive action there was always a risk of collision.

When an attack was conducted in a single 'line-ahead' formation getting back into Vs for the return flight often proved difficult. This was due to increasing confusion in the target area as successive planes screamed down to drop their bombs. The drill was for the leading planes to head back toward base at a speed which would enable the last aircraft in the line to catch up. Unfortunately the speed was rarely slow enough and the only alternative was to circle round in the target area. Stukas were especially vulnerable in such circumstances and enemy fighters are known to have joined such a circle and shot down Ju87s in quick succession as they overtook them from the rear. The signal to form up and get into V formation for the return to base was normally given by the Wing commander (flying in one of the leading Stukas) either by waggling his wings or over the radio.

An overcast sky covered by heavy cloud was a boon to Stuka operations as it not only brought an element of surprise but also hampered enemy anti-aircraft activity. Enemy fighter

Right: The diving attack sequence demonstrated by two Ju87Bs. In the first photograph the aircraft are flying straight and level, in the second the lead machine's pilot has pulled up the nose and started to roll to port, and in the third he is almost on his back and ready to enter an almost vertical dive.

Above: The Ju87's rear gunner had a perfect view of the result of his pilot's bomb aiming, but it must have been quite an experience to be virtually lying on one's back staring at the blue sky, then swung on the inside of an arc and pressed in the seat as the aircraft pulled out of its dive. The shadowy line on the left of the photograph is the 7.92mm machine gun's barrel.

aircraft also found their task more difficult, but so did the German fighters protecting the Stuka mission.

The normal war load was a 250kg bomb carried in a crutch behind the radiator, and four 50kg bombs in racks under the wings. A bomb release button on the control column enabled the pilot to drop all the bombs together or separately. The crutch carrying the 250kg bomb was mounted on swing links which lowered and swung the bomb forward on release so that it cleared the airscrew arc. Depending on the target the bombs were fitted with impact or delayed action fuses; release height in a dive attack varied between 600 and 1000m and in a level attack not less than 200m. (This was the minimum safe altitude, determined by the time between release and bomb detonation.) Successive dive bombers had to release their bombs at virtually the same height, for if a pilot dropped his bomb too soon the explosion would endanger the aircraft in front. Stukas operating in close support of ground troops usually dropped the 50kg wing bombs first as they were almost invariably of the high fragmentation variety.

The three basic forms of attack have been briefly described. The average *Sturzangriff* (nose-dive) attack was launched from an altitude of 4000m, a *Schrägangriff* (oblique) dive usually began at an average altitude of 800m. However every operation was determined by factors which varied according to the situation, such as surprise, atmospheric conditions and, above all, the enemy's anti-aircraft defenses; but experience proved that an effective dive-bombing attack could not be launched from an altitude of less than 2000m.

Radio communication was kept to the minimum throughout a Stuka mission. Generally it was used only to assist in target recognition prior to the attack and to help damaged machines on the return flight. Otherwise chatter on the air was frowned upon as likely to bring trouble in its wake. Instructions couched in obscure and indefinite terms passed over the planes intercom sometimes brought trouble also. On one occasion a Stuka pilot, irritated by the constant buzz in his ears emanating from the intercom, ordered his gunner in the rear cockpit to switch it off (*abstellen*). Seconds later the pilot and the crews of the other Stukas flying in formation with him saw the gunner parachuting to earth; he had understood that he was to jump (*abspringen*).

On completion of a mission, with the planes in their dispersal area being serviced and refuelled for the next sortie, there would be a squadron debriefing, the results of which would be passed on to the Wing commander and to whomever had ordered the operation.

Training

In 1939 it was accepted that it took six months to train a Stuka pilot but by the end of the war pilots were only getting about two months training and their quality deteriorated in consequence. Initial bomb-dropping training, with concrete-filled bombs, was done flying solo. The approach altitude at

Below: Fitted with underwing gondolas carrying two 37mm Flak 18 (BK 37) cannons, the G-1 was a formidable weapon achieving tremendous success in tank-busting on the Eastern Front. The G-1 was modified from the D-5 and the cannons could be removed and replaced by bomb racks.

which the dive should begin and the release point of the bombs on to a simulated target were both prescribed before the flight. These requirements were relatively simple when the training started – a straight flight at an altitude of 2500m with an approach against the wind and a simple shallow dive, for example. But as the training progressed, more stringent conditions were imposed until the pilot had completely mastered the necessary cockpit drill. Another phase of the training concentrated on strafing, with both pilot and rear gunner shooting at patterns of plates laid out on the ground. Finally, when both pilot and gunner were judged to have reached a certain standard of proficiency they would be trained to fly as part of a team, participating in simulated attacks by flights, squadrons and Wings.

Action: Attacks on Bridges

Attacks by Ju87s were launched against bridges on numerous occasions. Being relatively small precision targets, highly accurate bombing was called for – hence the use of Stukas. Being nodal points in the enemy's communication system anti-aircraft artillery was often deployed around them, but if they were undefended the customary form of attack was lengthways, into the wind if this was feasible. The effect of the bombs largely depended on the construction of the bridge. Unless a vital support was demolished, steel bridges could often withstand a number of direct hits. Attacks on wooden and pontoon bridges were usually more successful, but the Russians were adept at the quick repair of wooden structures. The heaviest bombs available (500kg) were invariably used. For steel and iron structures they were fitted with impact fuses; delayed action fuses were used when the target was a pontoon bridge as it was found that the bombs would create more damage after smashing through the pontoons and exploding in the water below.

In the summer of 1942 Stukas of I/StG2 attacked the wooden bridge which spanned the Don at Kalatsch. As heavy Soviet anti-aircraft fire was expected, the approach was made at an altitude of 3500m. A strong crosswind upset the trajectories of the bombs. Nevertheless the bridge received a number of direct hits in the first sortie and Soviet vehicles on the road nearby were destroyed. One squadron now turned its attention to the anti-aircraft guns, while the rest of the Wing put in a second attack on the bridge. This effectively knocked out the anti-aircraft defenses as the Russian gunners ceased firing as soon as the Stukas screamed down on their positions to drop impact bombs fused with Dinort sticks.

Attack on Trains and Railroad Installations

The bombing of railroad tracks running through open country was not usually considered to be a profitable enterprise and attacks of this nature were rarely undertaken. On occasions, however, when the disruption of railroad traffic was of paramount importance, Stukas dropped delayed-action 500kg bombs on the lines, flying up the track and selecting a point where the lines bridged a culvert or where there was a shunting junction. In September 1941 Stukas of I/StG2 based at Velish, 300 miles south of Leningrad, bombed the Moscow–Riga line near Velikye Luki in order to stop the Soviet reinforcements reaching the northern front. The terrain was flat and open, there were no anti-aircraft guns in the area and the operation was completed without interference

Above: The installation of the 37mm Flak cannon in its underwing gondola is very clear in this pleasing picture of a G-1. The ground crew are turning over the massive Jumo 211 twelve-cylinder engine.
Above right: This drawing of a G-1 captioned *Panzerbrecher* (Tank breaker) appeared on the cover of *Der Adler* in April 1944 in support of an article describing the aircraft's success against armor.
Below: This G-1 shows the location of the removed dive brakes.

from Soviet fighter aircraft. The Stukas simply circled round at an altitude of 6000m and leisurely dropped delayed action bombs at places where the collapse of the railroad embankment cut the track and made its repair more difficult.

Attacks on trains were usually more effective – and certainly more spectacular – than the disruption of open railroad lines. For such train-busting operations Stukas would carry a war load of one 250kg delayed action high-explosive bomb and four 50kg fragmentation bombs. The altitude of approach, which was usually made down the line, depended largely on whether or not there was any anti-aircraft fire. As a second attack was rarely possible the bombs were released singly during a shallow dive.

Some Stuka units specialized in knocking out armored trains. In February 1942 for example, Stukas of I/StG2 attacked a Soviet armored train operating on the Staraya Russa–Bologoye railroad some 200 miles south of Leningrad. The train was a thorn in the flesh of the German troops operating in the area, so they had appealed to the Luftwaffe. The attack was launched in daylight, in clear winter weather and into the wind, with the Stukas making steep dives on the moving train from an altitude of 300m. There was heavy flak but the bombs were accurately placed and six of the long armored carriages were seen to topple off the rails. No sooner had the Stukas returned to base, however, than a message was

Below: **An armorer loads up the 37mm cannon of a Ju87G-1. This powerful gun greatly improved the Stuka's tank-busting capabilities.**

received from the army with a plea for another strike. Six coaches had indeed been knocked off the rails but the Russians inside were still shooting, while the engine and one coach which remained on the line had pulled away from the wreckage. Having refuelled and bombed up the Stukas returned to the attack. This time Soviet fighters were waiting for them. Nevertheless the Stukas completed their mission and silenced the train.

Of all the efforts to upset enemy communications, attacks on the installations and facilities at railroad stations often had the most disruptive effect. Combined Luftwaffe bombing forces were sometimes used for strikes of this nature. In February 1942 for example, Stukas of I/StG2 and II/StG2, with a Wing of Heinkel He111 medium bombers under an umbrella of German fighters, attacked Bologoye station on the Moscow–Leningrad line. It was not a very successful operation. The Heinkels, flying well below the Stukas, dropped their bombs and the Stukas screamed in to complete the devastation. However the timing was awry and a strong wind was blowing across the target. Consequently with the Heinkels' bombs exploding as they dived into heavy flak and the wind blowing them off course, the Stukas' bombs were badly placed.

Attacks on Ships

To the majority of Stuka pilots ships were the most rewarding targets of all. The bombs carried by a single Stuka were capable of sinking a merchant ship or even a small warship, and the combined weight of bombs carried by a Stuka Wing was enough to sink a battleship. The movements and speed of a

Above: An armorer makes final checks to the 37mm cannon gondola. The slotted protrusion is the ejector chute for spent cartridge cases.
Right: Business end of the powerful 37mm cannon fitted to the Ju87G-1. The fairing above the mechanic's left shoulder covers the barrel aperture for the removed 7.92mm MG17.

ship, and the fact that the wind never seemed to favor the airman, often made the bombers' task a difficult one; moreover every warship bristled with anti-aircraft guns. Where to start the dive and when to release the bombs was of crucial importance when attacking a ship. Starting too soon and releasing the bomb too high invariably meant missing the target. Thus Stuka pilots were trained to approach an enemy ship at an altitude of between 3500 and 4500m, not to dive too steeply and to release their bombs as low as possible.

Some of the most successful Stuka attacks on shipping took place during the assault on Crete in May 1942. On 21 May an attempt was made to reinforce the German 7th Panzer Division on the island by sending in by sea units of the 5th Mountain Division. The German convoy, consisting mainly of caiques and small craft, was attacked *en route* by a force of British warships whose presence was spotted by a German reconnaissance plane. A call for air support quickly brought a Wing of Stukas to the scene, but by the time they got there most of the caiques and small craft carrying the German troops had been sunk. An attack was launched but on this occasion the ships of the Royal Navy managed by skillful maneuvering to dodge the 500kg and 50kg bombs which the Stukas hurled at them.

However they were not so lucky when the Stukas returned to the battle after refuelling and loading up more bombs. Throughout that day and the next the Stukas operated round the clock, attacking, flying back to their base at the southern tip of Peloponnesus to refuel and rearm, and returning to launch yet more attacks. In this action three British cruisers, (HMS *Fiji*, HMS *Gloucester* and HMS *York*) and six destroyers (among them HMS *Kelly* captained by the late Lord Louis Mountbatten) were sunk.

Tank Busting
Tanks, being relatively small objects, were the most difficult of the Stuka pilots' targets. Moreover to knock them out a direct hit was essential; near-misses rarely had much effect except perhaps to disable the tank temporarily. Attacks went in from the side with a shallow dive approach. The bombs which were employed were fitted with impact fuses and if they were released too low the result was a huge crater at the side of the tank, but – except to frighten the crew perhaps –

there was no other effect. Too level an approach resulted in the bomb taking a curved path over and around the tank. All in all therefore the results of bombing attacks on individual tanks were disappointing. Concentrations of tanks, forming up for an operation or refuelling, offered more chance of success but such targets were rare. Only when the Ju87G-1 carrying two 37mm Flak 18 cannons was introduced did Stuka tank-busting operations enjoy a measure of success, although a 'kill' largely depended on hitting the vehicle where the armor did not provide full protection. Apart from being more effective the cannon had one other great advantage. Enemy tanks which penetrated German defensive localities obviously could not be bombed out but they could be shot up.

One of the rare occasions when a concentration of tanks provided the target which could be classed as a Stuka bomber's dream was in June 1940. Twenty or thirty French tanks were spotted in a wood and a Wing of Stukas was called on to deal with them. The Stukas attacked and plastered the wood with bombs. When German troops reached the wood they found six burned-out tank hulks.

Attacks on Enemy Artillery and Infantry
Concentrations of vehicles were especially vulnerable targets and once the enemy had experienced a Stuka attack he was quick to seek safety in dispersal and camouflage. Stukas catching a column of vehicles on the move would usually fly a level course or attack in a series of shallow dives to enable the rear gunner to make maximum use of his machine gun.

Against artillery positions 50kg bombs were the most effective. The main problem in a strike against such targets was that of finding them. Gun pits were usually very well camouflaged and when the Stukas were in the area the guns would cease firing, so as not to reveal their exact location. To a lesser extent the same problem existed with infantry positions, against which the smaller fragmentation bombs were more effective.

DEVELOPMENT AND P[

Late in 1939 the Ju87B-2 succeeded the Ju87B-1 on the assembly line. Basically the same as the Ju87B-1, it incorporated a number of refinements. These included ejector exhausts, hydraulically-operated radiator cooling gills and an improved airscrew. When flown as a single seater the Ju87B-2 could carry a 1000kg bomb load. Subsequent modifications to both the B-1 version and the B-2 resulted in the Ju87B-1/U2 and the Ju87B-2/U2. These differed from their predecessors only insofar as they were equipped with improved radio equipment. The Ju87B-2/U3 which followed was intended specifically for close-support sorties, and was simply a Ju87B-2/U2 with additional armor protection. The Ju87B-2/U4 had skis instead of the usual wheeled undercarriage. Fitted with sand filters, yet another version of the B-2 was designated Ju87B-2/Trop. Both it and the standard Ju87B-2 were supplied to Italy's *Regia Aeronautica* and were flown by the Italian *Gruppi Tuffatori* (Dive Bomber Wing) on operations in the Balkans, Mediterranean and North Africa. Other Ju87B-2s were supplied to the Bulgarian, Hungarian and Rumanian air forces and subsequently saw operational service on the Russian front.

The Ju87C, another offshoot of the Ju87B, was the naval version of the Stuka. In 1938 the German Navy had no aircraft carriers, but one was under construction in Hamburg; when it was launched it was to be named *Graf Zeppelin*. During that year the Navy's High Command decided that the *Graf Zeppelin*'s air component should include a squadron of dive bombers and Junkers undertook to modify the current production Stuka for this purpose. The first prototype of the Ju87C-0 was produced in the summer of 1939. To make the plane more compact the outer wings folded back, it had arrester gear, an undercarriage which could be jettisoned in the event of an emergency landing on water and flotation equipment. The intention was that the production models which were to follow, designated Ju87C-1s, would feature additional modifications including an electrically-operated wing-folding mechanism, extra fuel tanks in the wings and fitments enabling a torpedo to be carried below the fuselage.

In the event the policy of the German High Command underwent a change in 1940, the *Graf Zeppelin* was never completed, work on the Ju87C-1s was halted and they were converted on the assembly line to Ju87B-2s.

Meanwhile in December 1938 a naval Stuka squadron which was to serve in the *Graf Zeppelin* had been formed at Kiel-Holtenau and the personnel had started to train on Ju87As. In September 1939 the prototype Ju87C-0s were handed over to this squadron, now known as the *4(Stuka) Staffel der Trägergruppe 186*, and brought up to strength with Ju87B-1s. The squadron was then attached to II/StG2 and subsequently saw service in the Polish campaign.

Being a naval air squadron it was to be expected that the 4(St)TrGr186 would be employed against targets of predominantly naval significance. The Polish naval base at Hela

Above: **A very prominent feature of the B and R versions was the oil-cooler intake on top of the cowling behind the propeller. This intake was not symmetrical about the center line, a feature made very clear by the lighting on this particular photograph.**

RODUCTION

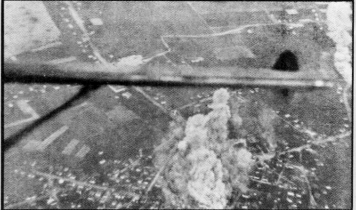

Above: Dive bombers were very effective for pinpoint attacks not only on armor and military installations but also communication systems. This Ju87 has just scored what looks to be a direct hit on a road, thus causing problems in bringing forward support and supplies to the front line.
Above left: The *Graf Zeppelin*, Germany's first aircraft carrier, being launched in December 1938.

Below: A perfect profile of the lines of the B and R versions. In this case the aircraft is a R-2 of StG1 flying without wing tanks but with two 110-lb bombs on the wing racks. The fins of a 550-lb bomb being carried on its center-line cradle can be seen behind the undercarriage legs. The werke number 6117 is painted in white on the rudder.

Below left: A Staffel of Ju87Bs fly over hostile looking terrain. The rod from the wing of the photographic aircraft in the foreground is the pitot tube which operates the aircraft's air speed indicator.
Right: A newly produced Ju87B-1; at least that is what it seems, but close examination shows that it is in fact one of the few Ju87C-Os built with manually folding wings and arrestor gear – visible just forward of the tail wheel – for use on the proposed aircraft carrier *Graf Zeppelin*. Most of the aircraft built were converted to B-2 standard or used for experimental work after building of the carrier was abandoned.

was bombed repeatedly, while returning from a mission there one of the squadron's Ju87C-0s was damaged by anti-aircraft fire. Anticipating having to land his aircraft in the sea, the pilot activated the explosive bolts which jettisoned the undercarriage. However it turned out that an emergency landing was not necessary and the pilot nursed the machine back to base where he made a belly landing. The incident was widely quoted by proponents of the Ju87 as evidence of the rugged toughness of the plane.

When production of the Ju87C-1 was stopped the Ju87C-0s were withdrawn. Subsequently, however, some of them were used in experimental trials. The most interesting were those conducted at Treuburg in 1944 with an 8cm smooth-bore recoilless gun mounted underneath the fuselage.

Production of the Ju87R series of Stukas started about the same time as that of the Ju87B-2. The suffix 'R' – an abbreviation of *Reichweite* (Range) – denoted the extended range of this version of the plane. The Ju87R was basically the same as the Ju87B-2, but it was equipped with an extra fuel tank in each wing and fitted to carry two disposable drop tanks under the wings in place of the underwing bomb racks. The capacity of the fuel tanks of the Ju87B-2 was 106 Imperial gallons; that of the Ju87R, when the drop tanks were carried, was 300 Imperial gallons. This increased the range from 600km to 1800km, and enabled the Ju87R to be used on antishipping operations and other long-range missions. The payload was reduced because of the extra fuel and only a single 250kg bomb could be carried. The first production planes of the R series were known as Ju87R-1s. Later versions, the Ju87R-2, Ju87R-3 and Ju87R-4, were simply modified versions of the Ju87R-1 – the modifications being mainly concerned with the aircraft's radio equipment. The first Ju87R-1s came off the production line early in 1940 and were issued to the Immel-

mann Wing (I/StG1) prior to the German invasion of Norway in April that year.

During 1940 the Ju87 was redesigned around a new Jumo 211J-1 engine, which had an induction air cooler, a shrouded supercharger impeller, a new boost and injection pump control and a pressurized cooling system. For takeoff this engine could develop 1400hp, and at an altitude of 4500m, 1410hp at 2700rpm. In the redesign of what was to become the Ju87D an attempt was made to improve the aircraft aerodynamically. The oil cooler was moved from the top of the engine cowling to a place below the cowling previously occupied by the cooling radiator, which was moved to a position below the center wing section. The old cockpit canopy was redesigned to reduce drag, the size of the undercarriage struts was reduced, the vertical tail surfaces were enlarged and provision was made for extra fuel tanks on the lines of the Ju87R.

The new design also provided for the fitting of additional armor around the positions occupied by the crew. The pilot's seat, shielded in front by a 10mm plate, was itself armored with plates 4mm and 8mm thick, as was the floor of the cockpit. The rear gunner was similarly protected by armored head and side plates. The two fixed forward-firing 7.92mm MG17 machine guns were retained, but the solitary MG15 machine gun mounted in the rear cockpit was replaced by twin MG17s; these, in turn, were subsequently replaced by a

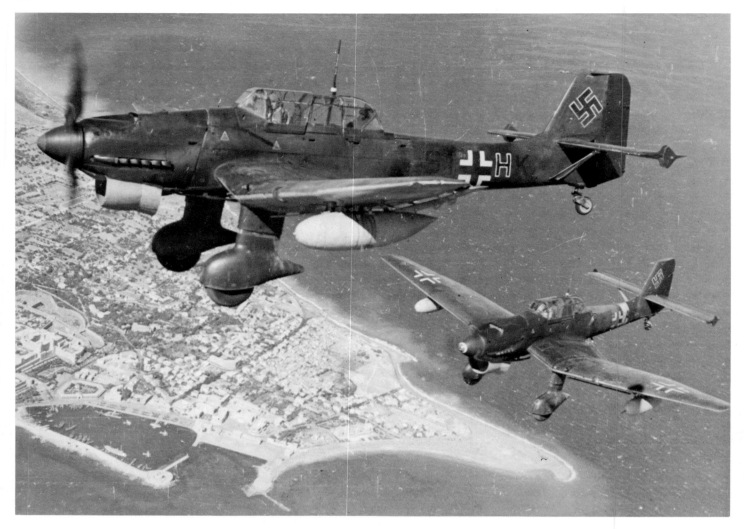

Above: **These two R-1 versions belong to the 2nd Staffel of StG3 and are being flown solo over Trapani, Sicily in 1941. The R-1 can often be identified by the absence of siren fairings on the undercarriage legs, but this is not entirely foolproof.**

pair of 7.92mm MG81s. The maximum bomb load was raised to 1800kg, although the Ju87D-1 normally carried either one 1000kg fragmentation or one 1400kg armor-piercing bomb. The racks under the wings could each take a single 500kg or a 250kg fragmentation bomb – or two of the 50kg general purpose bombs. In fact Ju87Ds operated by army co-operation close-support Wings often filled the wing racks with *Waffen-behälter* (weapon containers) containing machine guns and ammunition for dropping to the troops.

In the spring of 1941 the Ju87D-1 started to roll off the assembly lines and production of the Ju87B-2 was phased out. The Luftwaffe was looking for a new generation of high-performance aircraft and the way the war was progressing it was felt that the production of Stukas could be restricted. Indeed it was. In January 1941 seventy Ju87s were delivered to the Luftwaffe but only twelve were delivered that September and a mere two in November. However by then the war in the USSR had taken a turn for the worse and from that front came sharp demands for increased air support and replacements for the losses that had been suffered. Moreover it was apparent that it would be some considerable time before any of the new high-performance aircraft became available in quantity. So Stuka production was stepped up with a factory at Bremen augmenting the production of the Berlin-Tempelhof plant. Total production of Ju87s in 1941 was 476 and output was

almost doubled in 1942 when 917 Stukas were delivered to the Luftwaffe.

The Ju87D-1 started to be delivered to the *Stukagruppen* in the USSR early in 1942 and, as the Ju87D-1/Trop, it arrived in North Africa about the same time. From then on the Ju87Ds gradually replaced the older Ju87B-2s in the operational squadrons. Deliveries of the Ju87D-1 were supplemented with a variation, the Ju87D-2 – the only difference between the two planes being that the rear of the fuselage of the Ju87D-2 was reinforced and a stronger tailwheel assembly fitted so that it could be used as a cargo glider tug. The Ju87D-2 was employed mainly in North Africa and the Mediterranean Theater.

By the middle of 1942, however, with enemy fighter opposition increasing on all fronts Stuka operations were becoming more hazardous. Nevertheless it was considered that they still had a role to play, especially in close support of ground operations. By the end of 1942 yet another version, the Ju87D-3, was being produced. This plane was intended primarily for the *Schlachtgeschwader* (close-support group) and, although it was very similar to the Ju87D-1, and was

Top right: **This Italian operated R-1 carries yellow recognition bands around the nose and rear fuselage. This aircraft belongs to 239a** *Squadriglia* **of** *Bombardieri a tuffo Gruppo* **96° which was active in the Middle East.**
Center right: **The shape of the cockpit or 'glasshouse,' as it was known, is clearly defined in this pleasant side view of an R-2 of StG1. The later D and G versions had a much improved profile with the rear end of the cockpit sloping quite considerably.**
Right: **A Ju87R-2 of an Italian unit showing the extended dive brakes underneath the wings, and the long-range tanks.**

Above: Italian armorers unload a 500kg bomb from its delivery trolley. The jack was also used to position the weapon on the aircraft's center-line bomb cradle.

fitted with dive brakes, there was additional armor protection for the crew, the engine and radiator. Three squadrons of the Rumanian Air Force (*Escadrille* 81, 82 and 83) which had been flying Ju87B-2s on close-support missions at the Eastern Front were among the Stuka units to be re-equipped with Ju87D-3s.

Some modified Ju87D-1s and Ju87D-3s, designated Ju87D-4s, were equipped to carry torpedoes and were intended for antishipping operations. In the event they never saw active service and were eventually reconverted back to Ju87D-3s. Meanwhile the wing loadings, resulting from the ever-increasing payloads which Stukas were being required to carry on operational sorties, were reaching a dangerously high level. This led to the production in 1943 of the Ju87D-5 – a Stuka with a bigger wing span (15m instead of the 13.8m of the Ju87D-3) and the same disposable undercarriage as was fitted

to the Ju87C-0. Some of the first Ju87D-5s produced had the same wing dive brakes as the earlier models but, as Stukas were now being employed almost entirely on close support operations, the fitting of dive brakes was discontinued.

The Ju87D-6 and Ju87D-7 were modified versions of the Ju87D-5. The Ju87D-7, developed specifically for night harassment operations, had a Jumo 211p engine which reached 1500hp for takeoff and 1410hp at 5000m and was fitted with special night flying equipment. Large flame-damper tubes carried the exhaust back over the wing, and 20mm MG151 cannons were substituted for the forward-firing MG17 machine guns under the wings. Like its predecessor, the Ju87D-5, the Ju87D-7 had a disposable undercarriage and no dive brakes were fitted. The final version of the 'conventional' Stuka was the Ju87D-8 which differed from the Ju87D-7 only in so far as it had no flame-damper tubes and lacked specialized night flying equipment.

In considering the sequential development of the Stuka, mention must now be made of the Ju87F and Ju187. Both were experimental attempts by the Junkers design department at Dessau to evolve a successor for the Ju87. The Ju87F design was based on the Ju87D air frame but had an extended wing, a stronger undercarriage, and it was to have been powered by the powerful Jumo 213 engine. However the design was rejected by the German Air Ministry's *Technisches Amt* in the spring of 1941 on the grounds that the proposed new Stuka was only marginally better than the Ju87Ds, which were just about to come into service.

So the Junkers design team initiated a study which eventually culminated in the Ju187 design. Like its predecessors

Above: A D-1 of StG1 chases its shadow just prior to landing. The bomb cradle is empty and what appears to be the 'diving whistle' on the starboard undercarriage leg is in fact a 16mm camera.

Above left: A pair of Bf109Fs escort a quintet of Ju87D-1s believed to belong to StG3. Rear defensive armament was increased to a pair of 7.92mm either MG17s or MG81s. Close examination reveals this increased firepower on the first aircraft.

Below: This B-2 came to grief landing in Norway. The wooden sled was probably used to raise the cockpit in an effort to reach the crew, as well as a means of transporting the aircraft. The front parts of the wheel spats have been removed.

the projected new machine would retain the gull-like shape that distinguished the Stuka. The Ju187 had a fully retractable undercarriage, the two main struts of which folded back through 90 degrees and swung aft into wells in the wing. A remote-controlled turret aft carried one machine gun and one 20mm cannon, fixed forward-firing armament comprised two 20mm cannons. The maximum bomb load consisted of one 1000kg bomb under the fuselage and four 250kg bombs in racks under the wings. When the design was submitted to the German Air Ministry at the beginning of 1943 it was envisaged that the plane would be powered by a Jumo 213A engine capable of developing 1776hp for takeoff and 1480hp for climb and combat at 600m. However, as the maximum speed when it was fully loaded was not expected to exceed much over 400kph the design was turned down and the Ju187 project was finally abandoned in the autumn of 1943.

The Ju87G, to which reference has already been made, was the Stuka tank-buster. The Ju87G-1 was actually a converted Ju87D-3, equipped with a pair of 37mm Flak18 cannon below the wing, fitted just outside the main undercarriage. It was first tried out operationally in the summer of 1942 by several pilots, including Hans-Ulrich Rudel – the Stuka ace who was subsequently to make his name as the most famous of the Luftwaffe's tank-busters. Those who flew the modified Ju87D-3 were enthusiastic about its performance, and more Ju87D-3s were converted and redesignated Ju87G-1s. The first of these Stuka tank-busters arrived on the Eastern Front in October 1943 and tank destroyer squadrons were formed – one such squadron being added to each Stuka group.

As a tank destroyer the Ju87G-1 performed well. However it was a slow machine, difficult to maneuver and relatively easy prey for fighter aircraft. This eventually led to it being replaced in the army co-operation close-support groups by the Focke-Wulf FW190 for daytime operations. By the autumn of 1944 only one Wing (Rudel's III/StG2) equipped with Ju87Ds and Ju87Gs, and two antitank squadrons equipped with Ju87Gs, were operating by day.

Starting in 1943 a number of Ju87Ds were modified to become dual-control training aircraft and were designated Ju87H. The close-support Wings were suffering heavy casualties on the Eastern Front. With the Ju87Hs it was possible to speed up the conversion training of former fighter and bomber pilots who were remustered as Stuka pilots. Ju87D-1, D-3, D-5, D-7 and Ju87D-8 machines were all modified to become Ju87H-1, H-3, H-5, H-7 and Ju87H-8s respectively. Bomb racks and machine guns were removed, but apart from the installation of dual controls and the fitting of a new rear

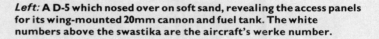

Left: **A D-5 which nosed over on soft sand, revealing the access panels for its wing-mounted 20mm cannon and fuel tank. The white numbers above the swastika are the aircraft's werke number.**

Above: **There is much of interest in this fine view of a Sicilian based Ju87R-1. The dive brakes are fully retracted, the wing racks are empty and the undersurfaces of the wings are (unusually) clear of all markings. The fairings covering the barrels of the two wing-mounted 7.92mm MG17 machine guns are clearly visible outboard of the undercarriage legs.**

Above: A captured Ju87G-1 is examined by American personnel in the closing days of World War II. The streamlined canopy of the G is particularly well shown. Another interesting feature is the 'soft' line between the camouflage colors; on Luftwaffe aircraft this was more usually a hard stencilled line.

Right: The Ju87 was a very big aircraft as can be seen by the scale added to this view of a D-5 by the two mechanics. Individual aircraft identity letters were often painted on wheel spats which also provided useful areas for other markings, both official and unofficial.

cockpit canopy which enabled the instructor to have more of a forward view, there was no difference between the H version and the corresponding D model.

Finally, a brief summary of the facts relating to the production of Stukas during World War II seems appropriate at this point. (A table detailing production figures of all the close-support aircraft in service with the Luftwaffe between 1939 and 1945 is reproduced as Appendix 3.)

It will be recalled that at the beginning of the war there were nine *Stukagruppen* in existence, equipped with some 336 Ju87Bs. Scattered around the training units were approximately 120 of the older Ju87As – many of which were probably no longer serviceable. A total of 134 more Stukas came off the 'Weser' assembly line during 1939, and 603 in 1940. Production dropped to 500 in 1941 but thereafter it increased in leaps and bounds, a total of 1072 being delivered to the Luftwaffe in 1943, peak monthly production was attained in March of that year. By the early summer of 1944, however, production was running down and it finally terminated in September that year, by which time a total of more than 5400 Ju87s had been manufactured.

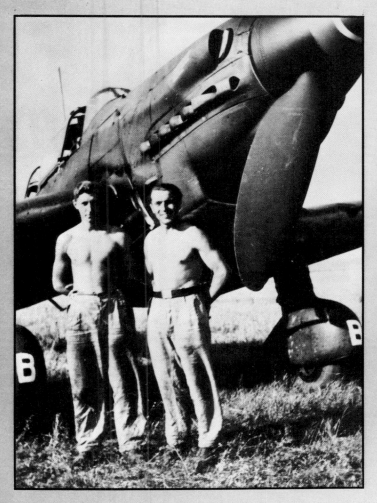

Below: The enormous propeller and its motive power, in this case a Junkers Jumo 211J-1 twelve-cylinder liquid cooled engine, are well to the fore in this shot of a D-8. This version of the Ju87 was fitted with wing-mounted 20mm MG151 cannon in place of the usual 7.9mm machine guns and the dive brakes were removed. A similar version for nocturnal use, in which flame dampers were fitted to the exhausts, was designated D-7.

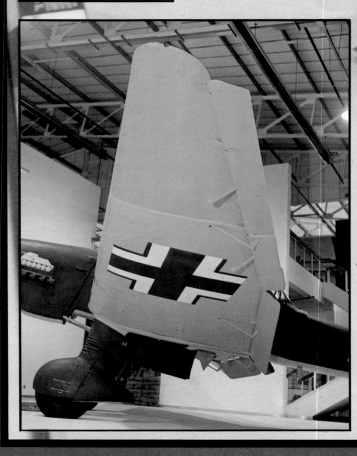

Junkers factory records show that 5709 Ju87s of all types were produced while Luftwaffe receipts show that 4881 were taken on charge. From this total only two complete aircraft survive, one in the United States and the other in England. The aircraft in America is a Ju87B and was restored in 1974 by the Experimental Aircraft Association of Wisconsin. The one in England is a Ju87D, which was restored by the RAF at St Athan and is now on display in the RAF Museum at Hendon. The history of the aircraft at Hendon is obscure and it is believed to have seen service on the Eastern Front, when fitted with two 37mm underwing cannons it was in the G-1 configuration. The series of color photographs reproduced here show it in its original D-5 form without the cannons. The work number is 494083 and although it is currently in the Battle of Britain display it carries the yellow tactical markings associated with the campaign in the east.

The rear defensive armament would be more correct if it showed two 7.92mm machine guns. Also there are no dive brakes under the wings, these being omitted from the D-5 and G models.

The white tank on the cowling is indicative of its tank-busting role which earned it the name of *Panzerknacker*. The yellow triangle below the cockpit indicates the octane rating of the fuel, and the small red cross shows the stowage position for the first-aid equipment.

The individual code letter J is painted in the *staffel* color, which in this case is shown by the K to be the 2nd *Staffel* which would form part of I *Gruppe*. The code R1 is an unrecorded *Geschwader*.

1

1. A Ju87G with one 37mm (BK 37) cannon (anti-armor) beneath each wing.
2. Luftwaffe bomber crews wore a one-piece protective flying suit over their uniforms. This Stuka crewman is also wearing a standard issue flying helmet and an 'other ranks' brown leather belt. The canopy belongs to a Ju87B-1 and illustrates the method of entry to the gunner's position.
3. Some neat formation flying by the pilot of the camera aircraft brings all the detail of armored canopy, engine cowling, armament and modified undercarriage of this G-1 into sharp perspective. The tank is a caricature of the Russian T-34 and appeared on most Ju87s of 10(Pz)SG1.
4. Internal cockpit framing, padded crash bar, and gunsight of the Ju87B are very clear in this view of one of the crew preparing for takeoff.

1. If the propeller of this Ju87D was spinning fast enough to render it completely invisible, the pilot would be unable to adopt the position he has, and the mechanic on the wheel spat would certainly not be able to retain his hat! This all points to a posed photograph which, nonetheless, shows the clear line of the D/G version top cowling, the familiar gull wing, and the enormous size of the aircraft.

2. An armorer carries a small bomb to the wing rack of a Ju87B-1. The forward firing 7.92mm wing-mounted machine gun can be seen above the wheel spat, the diving siren has been removed from its mounting which is fitted with a temporary cap.

3. The Ju-87R was basically a B with underwing tanks and increased fuel capacity in the wing cells which almost effectively doubled the range. This is an R-2 belonging to StG1 which was one of the first units to arrive in the Mediterranean in January 1941. The code more commonly associated with StG1 was A5.

4. A Ju87B of III/StG2 *Immelmann* which operated during the Battle of Britain period, 1940.

5. Colorful markings are often associated with Luftwaffe fighter *Geschwadern*, but this photograph of Ju87B-1s of II/StG77 photographed at Breslau-Schongarten in August 1939 shows this not to be the case. The sharks' teeth motif was popular with all air forces, especially on aircraft where a large chin radiator enabled them to be painted to the best effect.

6. Ground crew turn over the Jumo engine of a Ju87B-1. The exhaust system of this model was replaced by a much improved design from the B-2 onward.

7. This rather pleasing shot of a Ju87R-1 in Italian markings presents a good view of the wing tank, faired over wing mounted machine gun, chin radiator, and cooler intake. Unfortunately the fully castoring tail wheel has been clipped by the cameraman.

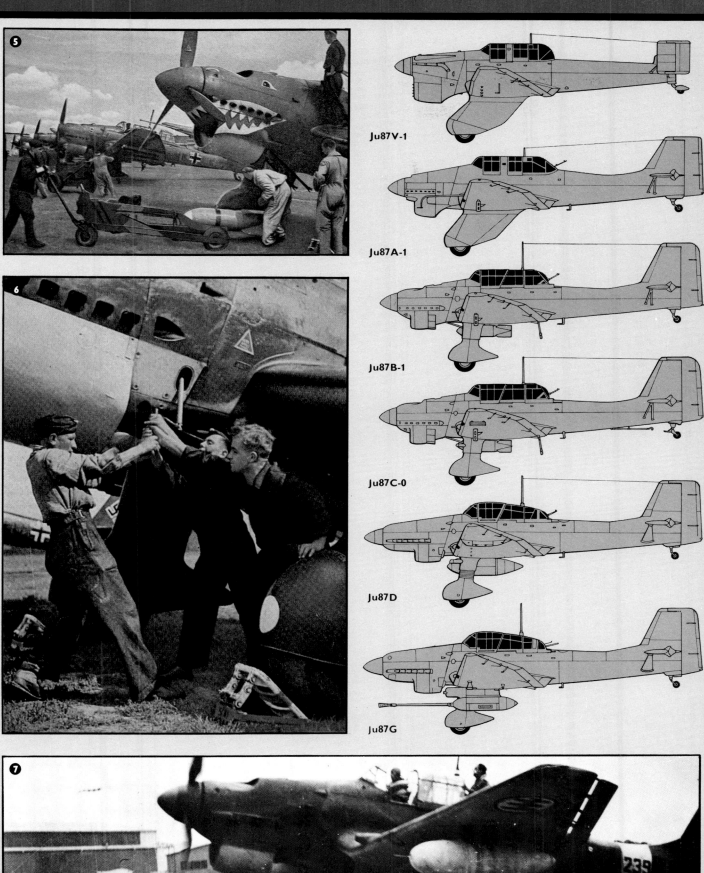

Ju87V-1

Ju87A-1

Ju87B-1

Ju87C-0

Ju87D

Ju87G

STUKA FORMATIONS A

Stukageschwader, like the Luftwaffe's fighter and bomber groups, generally consisted of three Wings. The Wings were deployed separately, and after the Battle of Britain groups rarely went into action as complete formations. Until the outbreak of World War II in 1939 the Wing was regarded as the basic formation and OKL (*Oberkommando der Luftwaffe*) and OKH (*Oberkommando des Heeres*) reports on Stuka actions in the Polish campaign refer not to Stuka Groups but to the deployment of nine and one third Wings. Only after the fall of France in 1940 were the *Stukagruppen* and *Schlachtflieger-gruppen* close-support Wings organized into *Geschwader* for the forthcoming invasion of Britain – Operation Sealion. By the time this project petered out *Stuka* and *Schlachtflieger* Groups had suffered heavy losses and after the Battle of Britain they never flew again on group missions – except on one occasion. The sole exception was *Stukageschwader* III, the formation supporting Rommel's Afrika Korps in the Western Desert, whose three Wings fought up to Alamein and back to Tunis.

Throughout the war – but especially in the first two years – the Stuka groups and *Schlachtflieger* squadrons were tremendously popular with the German Army. It was a popularity well deserved, for they were regarded as the army's 'fire brigade' to be called upon whenever the troops ran into difficulties. Although still organized into *Geschwader*, in Russia the Stuka Wings were deployed as separate units, possibly even in different theaters. (As commander of StG2 toward the end of the war, Hans-Ulrich Rudel com-

plained of the difficulties of administering a Stuka Group when one Wing was in Austria, another in the Sudetenland and the third in Czechoslovakia.)

In view of all the changes, transfers and cross-postings that were effected during the course of the different campaigns it is virtually impossible to trace the deployment and redeployment of the Stuka Wings with any accuracy. All that is possible is to record their positioning at the beginning of the more important campaigns. In September 1939, for example, an OKW report stated that all nine and one third of the Luftwaffe's *Stukagruppen* (that is nine Wings and one squadron) with a total of 366 Ju87A and Ju87B planes had been deployed for the attack on Poland. (Another source gives the *operational* Stuka strength as 219.) There was also a close support Wing equipped with forty Henschel Hs123s. Operating in the north were the *Luftflotte* 1's I/StG1, II/StG2 and III/StG2 together with the 4(St) *Trägergruppe* 186. Operating in the south were *Luftflotte* 3's III/StG51 and *Luftflotte* 4's I/StG76, I/StG77 and II/StG77 together with I/StG2 detached from *Luftflotte* 1. During the campaign 31 Stukas are said to have been lost.

In Poland the tool that had been forged in Spain really came into its own. According to Field Marshal Albrecht Kesselring much of the credit for the speed and success of the campaign could be attributed to the support provided by the Stukas, whose crews flew an average of four sorties a day. Whenever Guderian's armored columns ran up against opposition which could not be brushed aside the Stukas were called. They were

AT WAR

Above: Wolfram von Richthofen, commander of *Fliegerkorps* VIII.
Top left: The Ju87 suffered badly at the hands of the RAF during the Battle of Britain. This B-2 carries the badge of the 7th *Staffel* of StG1 and has the legend 'Lee On Solent' painted on the cowling. This is a legacy from the campaign over England since this particular aircraft was photographed in the Balkans. The rear canopy slid back toward the aircraft's tail to allow the gunner access. The pilot's canopy also slid rearward on runners, which are clearly visible.
Above left: This very clean looking Ju87 operating in North Africa carries fragmentation antipersonnel bombs on its wing racks. The dive sirens mounted on the spats have been removed, as have the wing mounted 7.92mm machine guns. Overall finish is sand, with light blue undersides, a white fuselage band and white wing tips.
Below: A Ju87 preparing to take off for a raid on Malta.

quickly on the scene and screeching down on the Poles blocking the German advance, with the fury which distinguishes the dive bomber. It was all too simple. The opposition folded up and the German Panzers rolled forward again. The campaign in Poland, observed Major General Fuller, was not decided by numerical superiority but by the speed with which the German tanks moved and the co-operation which existed between Panzer units and Luftwaffe.

Only one *Stukagruppe*, I/StG1, equipped with Ju87B-1s participated in the invasion of Denmark and Norway, but the invasion of France and the Low countries began before the end of the campaign in Norway and the bulk of the *Stukagruppen* were concentrated in *Fliegerkorps VIII*, under the command of Generalleutnant Wolfram von Richthofen. This was the same Freiherr von Richthofen who in July 1936 had ordered development work on the Ju87 to cease. Experience with the Condor Legion in Spain had caused him to change his mind about the Stuka and he became an army co-operation close-support specialist. Von Richthofen was a younger cousin of the famous World War I flier, in whose squadron he had served.

On 10 May 1940 von Richthofen had the following formations under his command: I/StG2 and III/StG2 to which I/StG76 had been attached, I/StG77 and II/StG77 to which IV(St)LG1 was attached and finally the II (Schlacht)LG2 – with a total strength of 342 Stukas and 42 Henschel Hs123s. This force supported by fighter squadrons constituted what would now be regarded as a tactical force. As such it was used with great success when the offensive started. The first call for assistance came during the assault on the Belgian fortress of Eben Emael, after that the Stukas were in action continuously, blasting ahead of the tank forces advancing toward the Atlantic coast, attacking enemy gun positions and flying to the limit of their range to strike at ships around Calais and Dunkirk. Despite the intensity of the operations, the attrition rate was

Above and right: The empty wings and fuselage racks indicates that these Italian operated Ju87Bs have completed a bombing mission, but the impeccable formation suggests that this is more likely to be a training flight. All four photographs graphically illustrate how prominent the fin and rudder marking used on Italian Ju87s was. The fuselage band is the white tactical marking associated with Axis aircraft used in the Middle East.

The aircraft flying on the extreme port side of the formation in the above center photograph is a D version as evidenced by its more streamlined canopy. The unit is 239° Squadron 97° *Gruppo* BaT based at Comiso.

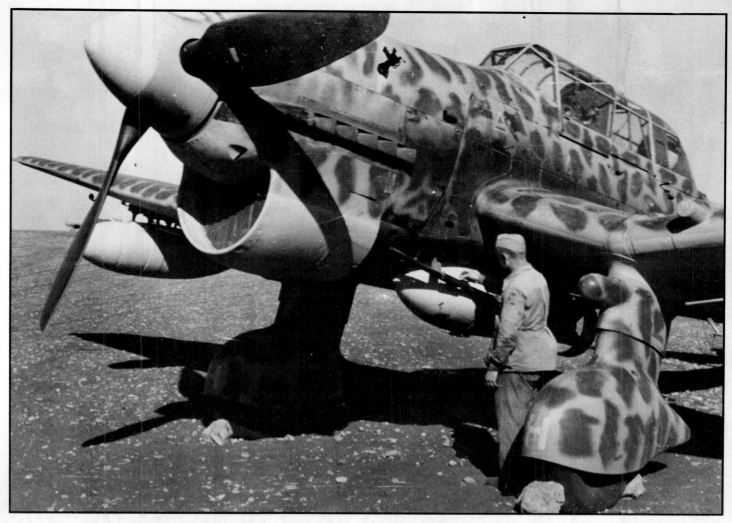

Above: The Ju87 appeared on every front in support of German land forces. This desert camouflaged aircraft of StG1 is an R version, which was basically a B with long-range wing tanks. The aircraft's range was increased by modified internal tankage as well as the 'wet' points which enabled two 66-imperial gallon tanks to be carried; the starboard one can be clearly seen. This aircraft has had its 7.9mm wing machine guns removed, and the attachment for the siren on the wheel spats has also been faired over.

comparatively low – only fourteen Ju87s were lost during the first week of the campaign.

During July, while the Luftwaffe was preparing for the great *Adlerangriff* (Eagle-attack) which was to mark the opening of the onslaught on Britain – Operation Sealion – the *Stukagruppen* were organized into *Geschwader*. Each was three Wings strong, and a new *Stukagruppe* I/StG3, was formed. The original naval unit, 4(St)TrGr 186, which had been brought up to full group strength during the campaign in Poland now became III/StG1. III/StG77 was redesignated II/StG1.

By mid-August 316 Ju87s were deployed for the assault on Britain, these belonged to II/StG1 and IV(St)LG1 under the command of Fliegerkorps II. Those of I, II and III/StG88 were under *Fliegerkorps* VIII. The first phase of what was to become known as the Battle of Britain started in June 1940 with attacks on shipping in the English Channel. From then on the Luftwaffe gradually extended its operations until the opening of the second phase – following the directive issued by Hitler on 2 August, ordering the war against Britain to be 'intensified.' The day appointed for the launching of the *Adlerangriff* was 10 August but the Luftwaffe did not open the main offensive until three days later, due to the weather and losses incurred in two great air battles near Dover and Portland. Casualties in the Stuka squadrons were mounting even before *Adlertag* and on 18 August III/StG77 lost no less than fourteen Ju87s in attacks on radar stations at Ford and on Thorney Island. It was clear that the Ju87s were unable to survive when attacked by British Hurricanes and Spitfires. To prevent the *Stukagruppen* from being decimated they were withdrawn to sit out the first phase of the Battle of Britain.

The Battle of Britain did not spell the end of the Stuka's

Below: **A wrecked D-2 of III/StG3 shares its last resting place with Bf109s. The S7 identifies** *Stukageschwader* **3, the T signifies a 9th** *Staffel* **aircraft and the G on the white tactical band is the aircraft's individual code letter.**

operational career, and it was to enjoy several more noteworthy successes before it became redundant. At the beginning of January 1941 two Stuka Wings – I/StG1 under Hauptmann Hozzel and II/StG2 under Major Ennecerus – moved to Sicily to attack Allied shipping in the Mediterranean. On 10 January 43 Stukas from these two formations attacked and seriously damaged the aircraft carrier *Illustrious*. Six days later HMS *Illustrious* was hit again during an attack on Malta's Valetta Harbor, but due to amazing effort on the part of the repairers she was able to slip out of the harbor four days later and get away without further mishaps. These successes, together with reports that Malta was suffering heavily from the constant hammering of the island's ports and airfields by the Stukas, led to two other *Stukagruppen*, II/StG1 and III/StG1, being dispatched to Sicily and North Africa. Meanwhile I/StG2, III/StG2 and III/StG51 together with I/StG3 (formerly I/StG76) and the close-support wings II were transferred from France for the onslaught against the Balkans. Thus in April 1941 von Richthofen's *Fliegerkorps* VIII could muster 414 Ju87s of which approximately 350 were operational; later these were augmented by 127 Ju87s of the three Wings of StG77.

During the campaigns in Yugoslavia and Greece the Luftwaffe enjoyed complete air superiority, so the *Stukagruppen* had ideal operating conditions. As soon as these campaigns had been successfully concluded the Luftwaffe's Stuka Wings operating from Peloponnesian airfields were unleashed on Crete to soften it up for Operation Merkur – the airborne invasion of the island. The airfields were pounded and a series of missions were launched in support of the German paratroops who had been dropped around Maleme. It was during the assault on Crete that the Stukas achieved some of their most spectacular successes. Flying from Molae, Mycenae and the island of Scarpanto between Crete and Rhodes, the three wings of StG2 Immelmann attacked HMS *Southampton* and HMS *Gloucester*, two cruisers escorting a convoy east of Malta.

Above: **The armored windshield of this Ju87B can be seen just above the badge of StG1. The wing-mounted machine gun fairing with the barrel protruding, can be seen between the headgear of the three mechanics in the foreground.**

Above left: **The large scoop for air to enter the machines' engine coolant system was another very prominent feature of all Ju87s. This view of an Italian aircraft being readied for a raid on Malta, illustrates it very well.**

Left: **A captured D-2 of StG3, in this case a 3rd *Staffel* I *Gruppe* aircraft, showing the wing racks, removed siren housings, and the wing-mounted machine guns.**

Below left: **The famous Bonzo Dog motif of StG1 is evident on the cowling of this Ju87D.**

Below: **The slipstream-driven dive-bombing propeller fitted to both wheel spats created a morale sapping screech as the Ju87 dived on its target. Once again the motif of StG1 and the 7.9mm machine-gun barrels are very much in evidence.**

Both ships were badly damaged and the *Southampton* had to be abandoned. During the next few days four destroyers – HMS *Juno*, HMS *Greyhound*, HMS *Kelly* and HMS *Kashmir* – were also sunk in Stuka attacks, and several other ships were severely damaged.

Meantime *Luftflotte* 2 had been moved to the Mediterranean to complete the task of crushing Malta and of supporting Rommel's Afrika Korps. From June 1941 three Wings of StG3 were operating mainly in North Africa and at a time when there was little fighter opposition they gave Rommel's men invaluable support. Highlights in their activities were the bombing of Tobruk in April 1942 and their contribution to the operations which compelled the Free French to evacuate the desert fortress of Bir Hacheim two months later. By the middle of 1942, however, as StG3 was converting from Ju87Bs to Ju87Ds, Allied air power in the Middle East was gaining strength. This, coupled with a shortage of fuel, led to a reduction in the operational capability of the Stuka and toward the end of the campaign in Tunisia the surviving Stukas were pulled back to Italy.

Prior to the invasion of Russia in June 1941, *Stukagruppen* were transferred from the Mediterranean and Balkan theaters. When Operation Barbarossa was launched some 200 serviceable Stukas from seven groups were available. They were supported by the Messerschmitt Bf 110s of the SKG210 (*Schnellkampfgeschwader*: literally High Speed Battle Group). These were old two-seater day and night fighters used in a ground attack role. In January 1942 the Stuka strength in Russia was augmented by two close support Wings, in 1943 by StG3 with three Wings, and in July 1944 by SchG4 with two Wings. There were also a few independent tank-busting squadrons and night harassment Wings (NSGr) operating throughout the Russian campaign.

Operation Barbarossa started well, and it seemed for a while that the campaign in Russia would be a repeat of the 1940 offensive in France and the Low Countries. There was little opposition in the air and the Stukas were able to roam freely over the battlefields. Purloining General Heinz Guderian's words 'Don't tickle with the finger, hit with the fist,' to express his views, von Richthofen massed his Stuka Wings and deployed them in strength as the tactical situation demanded. Kesselring, citing this use of concentrated air power, said later 'concentration of force even in difficult circumstances is the basis of victory. . . .'

The situation began to change in 1942 and by the end of that year the *Stukagruppen* in the USSR were finding it difficult to survive on daylight operations. After the battles of Stalingrad the Stukas were gradually relegated to a true fire brigade role – to be called upon only when no other form of support was available. At the beginning of 1943 the first *Stukagruppe* converted to the Focke-Wulf 190 and by October when the *Stukageschwader* were redesignated *Schlachtgeschwader*, squadrons still equipped with Ju87s were changing over to FW190s at the rate of two groups every six weeks. The Ju87s they surrendered went to the newly-formed *Nachtschlachtgruppen* (Night-Harassment Wings) and by late September 1944 only one Stuka group equipped with Ju87s was still engaged on daylight operations on the Eastern Front (this was Rudel's III/StG2).

On the Italian front two Wings of *Schlachtgeschwader 2* (SG2) operated until mid-October 1942; from June 1943 the three Wings of SG10 were deployed there until they were relieved by the three Wings of SG4. The SG4 continued to undertake daylight sorties until May 1944 when Rome fell. The Stuka's days were numbered, by the time the Allies landed in Normandy the Stuka had precious little chance of survival. Those Ju87s that remained (481, of which 319 were serviceable) were all assigned to the *Nachtschlachtgruppen*.

51

Above: The werke number, 494230, is painted very boldly across the top of the fin on this **G-1**. Note the absence of dive brakes and code letters under the wings. What seems to be a solid connection to the antenna is in fact the aircraft's pitot head which operated the air-speed indicator.

Top right: The 20mm cannon mounted in the wing positions on the **D-8** can be clearly seen on this aircraft serving on the Eastern Front.

Above right: Snow and slush combine to produce a treacherous surface for this Ju87D as it taxies to its takeoff point.

Right: Six Ju87s carry out a stream landing on a temporary airfield on the Eastern Front. The Bf 109 in the foreground has had its wheel doors removed to prevent snow clogging the undercarriage.

Below: A three-quarter rear view of an Italian operated Ju87B.

THE NIGHT HARASSME

In 1942 the Luftwaffe was technically if not also numerically superior to the Soviet Air Force, and Russian planes were rarely seen by day. However, during the German advance toward Moscow in the autumn of that year Soviet aviators in antiquated biplanes took to flying by night over the German lines, dropping flares, little fragmentation bombs and incendiaries. These caused little physical damage but the 'sewing-machine' raids – so called by the German troops because of the sound of the Soviet planes' engines – did cause the troops to lose sleep, upset supply arrangements and disturbed troop movements being carried out under cover of darkness.

In 1942 the Germans decided to respond in kind by raising *Störkampfstaffeln* (Harassment Squadrons) '. . . to harass the enemy by nocturnal assaults on area targets in the forward areas. . . .' The first squadrons were formed in October 1942 and allocated to *Luftflotte* 1 and 4 and to the Eastern Air Command. They were initially designated 'Auxiliary' squadrons but in November 1942 they reverted to the *Stör-*

kampfstaffel designation. All the squadrons were equipped with Henschel 45s, armed with one fixed forward-firing 7.92mm MG17 machine gun and one 7.92mm MG15 machine gun on a flexible mounting in the rear cockpit. The bomb load to begin with comprised 10kg fragmentation bombs but these were soon replaced by 50kg and 70kg incendiary and high-explosive bombs. Flying Training School instructors and the pilots of redundant short-range reconnaissance aircraft were drafted into the squadrons to pilot the Henschels; many of the observer/rear-gunner/bombers who flew in the rear cockpit were recruited from Luftwaffe ground staff and *Wehrmacht* personnel keen to get away from soldiering on the ground on the Eastern Front. Some of these rear-gunners had never flown before and their first flights were over Stalingrad where the factories constituted an important harassment target.

More *Nachtschlacht* (night harassment) squadrons were raised at the beginning of 1943 and by the spring there were thirteen of them in existence. In October 1943 they were re-

Below: This D-8 served with StG3 in Italy and shows clearly some of the main differences from earlier D models. There are no dive brakes, the wing armament is a pair of 20mm MG15s, the jettisonable undercarriage of the D-5 is retained and the improved wing racks can be seen inboard of the increased span tips.

NT WINGS

(Nachtschlachtgruppen NSGr)

grouped into six *Nachtschlachtgruppen* (NSG 1–6) of two squadrons (one Wing had three squadrons). In 1944 four more Wings were formed: NSG7 for service on the southeastern sector of the Eastern Front; NSG8 with *Luftflotte* 5 based in Finland and Norway, NSG9 with *Luftflotte* 2 in Italy; NSG10 raised in September joined NSG7 with *Luftflotte* I. Later two more Wings, NSG11 and NSG12, were raised for service in Estonia and Latvia respectively.

Together these twelve Wings saw considerable action on every front in every theater of war, from Latvia and Estonia down to Italy. By 1944 they were flying a whole variety of mainly obsolete and obsolescent aircraft. Apart from the original Heinkel 45s, there were He46s, Hs126s, Arado Ar66s, Arado Ar96s, old Gotha bombers, Focke-Wulf 58s, Dornier Do17s, Italian Fiat Fighters CR32s and CR42s, a few old Savoia-Marchetti bombers, some captured aircraft and, of course, the ubiquitous Ju87. Experience gained on the Eastern Front suggested that – after the Ju87 – the old slow-flying Arados and Gothas were best suited to night harassment missions. When the close-support Wings converted to Focke-Wulf 190, the Ju87s made available were fed into the *Nachtschlachtgruppen*. (NSG20, one of the last two NS Wings to be formed toward the end of the war was equipped with FW190s. This was because it was merely a redesignated Night-Fighter Wing. Similarly the NSG30 was formed from the remaining personnel of a former bomber group which already had Junkers Ju88s. Both NS Wings were to be employed in western Europe. However as there was barely any fuel in Germany by the time the NSG30 was ready to go into action, it never flew.)

To train the NS air crews a special night-flying school was set up. At that time none of the modern sophisticated aids which enable pilots to fly by instruments alone were available. Direction, distance and altitude had to be worked out and maintained solely by means of compass, altimeter, twin and level indicators. An extra dashboard light was fitted in the pilots cockpit to facilitate his instrument observation, and flare paths were laid on the landing strips from which the NS squadrons operated. However, the possibility of interference by enemy night fighters limited the use of the flares. Near the front in Russia the flares were sometimes laid out up to 30km from the landing ground. NS pilots returning from a mission having spotted the flares were then expected to know where to land. Not unnaturally only the more experienced pilots were able to cope with night flying of this nature, and the casualties among the younger pilots were very heavy.

Nevertheless, despite the heavy attrition rate, it was concluded that the activities of the NS squadrons upset the enemy and so eased the pressure on the ground troops. One of the NS Wings under Major Heinz Müller flew no less than 17,000 sorties, 500 of which were made over Europe after the Allied invasion of Normandy when the Allies had almost complete air supremacy. Finally it is appropriate to record one of the more noteworthy successes achieved by the NS Wings. This was the destruction of a road bridge over the Rhine by FW190s of NSG20 in a daylight attack. For the Allies this bridge was a vital communication link and although the attackers suffered very heavy casualties the cost was considered worthwhile.

RUDEL:THE STUKA AC

Above: Hans-Ulrich Rudel was the Luftwaffe's most famous tank-buster.
Left: Rudel in his flying gear, wearing his Knight's Cross with Oakleaves, Swords and Diamonds at the neck of his *fliegerblouse.*
Below: Rudel in his Ju87D.
Below right: Rudel poses for the camera with a colleague.

E

Although in retrospect it might be judged to have been already obsolete at the beginning of hostilities, the controversial Ju87 was one of the most successful warplanes of World War II. Credit for its record can be attributed largely to those who flew the Stukas. They were brave young men, few of them older than 28, who had something more than courage. They had that restless spirit of aggression, that passion to get to grips with the enemy which is the hallmark of the finest troops. Some, like Hans-Ulrich Rudel, Alfred Druschel and Ernst Kupfer were so fiercely possessed of this spirit, and of the skill to survive the dangers into which it drew them, that their names were quickly added to the immortal company of Immelmann and von Richthofen. All the Stuka pilots possessed it to a high degree, and it was this which laid the foundation of the almost legendary reputation which the Stuka acquired in the Polish and French campaigns.

Of all the Luftwaffe's air aces the most famous, the most adventurous and the most decorated was Hans-Ulrich Rudel. In less than four years – for it took him eighteen months to persuade his superiors that he was capable of piloting a Stuka on active service – Rudel flew 2530 sorties, and Stalin had put a price of 100,000 rubles on his head. He started the war as a humble lieutenant and finished it as a colonel, commanding the oldest and best known of the Stuka close-support groups – *Schlachtgeschwader* 2 Immelmann. By then he had also received all of Germany's highest awards for bravery. If Rudel were to be compared with Allied air heroes, Douglas 'Tin-Legs' Bader the famous British fighter pilot would bear the closest resemblance to him in outlook and experience.

Born in July 1916 in Silesia, Rudel was the son of a clergyman. As a small boy there was little to suggest that he was especially brave; indeed it is said that his mother had to hold his hand when it thundered. Nor did he seem to be particularly clever, but he was always fond of sport. Perhaps it was because he saw opportunities for developing his sporting activities in the fighting services that in 1936 he joined the Luftwaffe as an officer cadet. Having passed his flying training course and qualified as a pilot Rudel volunteered for further training in dive-bombing techniques. At that stage it seems clear that his instructors had no great regard for Rudel's ability, his request was turned down and – much to his chagrin – he was sent on an air reconnaissance observer's course. As a result he flew during the campaign in Poland not as a pilot, but as an observer on long-range reconnaissance missions. To Rudel, whose ambition was to be in what was then regarded by many of the young Luftwaffe pilots as the most glamorous branch of the service, flying Ju87s, this was a tedious job. His applications to transfer to the Stuka groups were repeatedly turned down until March 1940 when he was allotted a vacancy on one of the Ju87 flying training courses. Having completed this he was posted to a Stuka training Wing near Stuttgart, where Oberleutnant Rudel sat out the campaign in France and the Low Countries.

Rudel's problems at this time seem to have stemmed from the confidential reports written by the chief instructor of the school where he had learned to fly. 'Rudel,' wrote this officer, 'is a dull and stolid sort of individual – a strange chap whose only outside interest appears to be sport. He doesn't smoke,

drinks only milk, and has no girl friends. . . .' Unfortunately for Rudel, when he did eventually manage to get himself posted to a first-line Stuka formation (the 1/StG2), he found that the Wing's adjutant was none other than his erstwhile flying instructor. In consequence when the *Geschwader* was flying in support of the airborne invasion of Crete, Rudel found himself relegated to duties outside the battle zone. However, a chance to prove his worth presented itself when Operation Barbarossa was launched. I/StG2 moved to the Eastern Front and was flying sorties almost round the clock. Every air crew was needed and Rudel was posted to a squadron whose squadron leader took an instant liking to him. 'Rudel is the best man in my squadron,' he said two or three weeks later, 'but he's a crazy fellow who isn't likely to live very long!'

Rudel took off on his first dive-bombing mission at 0300 on the morning of 23 June 1941; he was still flying eighteen hours later, having been out on four separate missions. The tempo of operations was such that the Stuka pilots were sometimes required to fly up to eight sorties a day for weeks on end.

Rudel's greatest single achievement came in September 1941. Two Wings of his *Geschwader* had moved up to Tyrkovo, south of Luga, for the offensive directed against Leningrad. Toward the middle of the month a reconnaissance plane spotted the battleships *Aktyabr Revaluzija* and *Marat* together with a couple of cruisers and some lesser craft of the Soviet Baltic Fleet in Kronstadt harbor. The *Geschwader* decided to attack and three squadrons carrying special 1000kg bombs duly took off on the morning of 23 September. Rudel was piloting a Stuka of the leading flight, and when the attack went in he was directly behind the squadron leader who had said Rudel was 'a crazy fellow.'

According to Rudel it was a clear day – no cloud and a blue sky. At that stage of the war Soviet fighters were rarely seen and, true to form, none appeared on 23 September. The Stukas approached Kronstadt at an altitude of 3000m and about 15km from their target they ran into a storm of anti-aircraft fire. 'It was murderous,' said Rudel, 'the Ivans weren't shooting at individual planes, but putting up a barrage . . . if it hadn't been so dangerous I might have described it as a carnival in the air.' Some of the Stukas tried to evade the fire and in doing so the flights and squadrons got mixed up. However, Rudel's squadron leader resolutely stuck to his course with Rudel close on his tail. When Rudel saw his leader had actuated his plane's air brakes he did the same and both Stukas started their dive at an angle of between seventy and eighty degrees. Screeching down toward the *Marat*, Rudel saw that his leader was retracting his air brakes; as before he followed suit. The effect was dramatic; the air speed of both planes increased and to the obvious horror of the rear gunner in the leading plane, whose face was plainly visible to Rudel only a few meters behind, Rudel's plane started to overhaul the one in front. To Rudel there was only one thing to do: forcing the control stick forward he shot down at a steep angle, almost ninety degrees, and just cleared the Stuka in front. Now the *Marat* appeared to be rushing up toward him, and Rudel could see Russian sailors scurrying about on her deck. At 300m, with the ship squarely in his sights, Rudel pressed the bomb-release button and simultaneously pulled back hard on the control stick. Levelling out was difficult, for the acceleration was way above the acceptable limit and for a few seconds Rudel blacked out. When he came to his senses he found he was flying only three or four meters above the water and his excited rear gunner was shouting over the intercom 'We've got her . . . you must have hit her ammunition store.' It was true, photographs taken by one of the Stukas in the rear of the column showed that the *Marat* was finished.

In winter the nature of the war in Russia changed. The StG2 was operating in support of the German advance toward Smolensk at this stage and Rudel has described how difficult it was to keep the Stukas in action. By November the temperature at night had dropped to minus forty degrees centigrade, in December it was even lower – minus fifty degrees centigrade. Cold of this order brought a host of problems in its wake, technical problems with the machines, human problems with the men who maintained and flew them. Masses of snow, ice, pitch-black nights, fog and low-flying cloud exacerbated the problems. The ability of the Russians to cope with such conditions coupled with their going on to the offensive made the problems worse. Engines would not start, hydraulics would not work and the operational strength of the Stuka squadrons sharply declined. Eventually the engine trouble was overcome by starting up each Stuka every half hour, night and day, and by covering the cowlings with straw mats and blankets. But this entailed extra work for the ground personnel who were already overworked. Furthermore it resulted in a dramatic increase in frostbite casualties.

Flying conditions were equally deplorable. Returning from a reconnaissance in the winter of 1943–44 Rudel ran into a thick impenetrable fog over enemy territory. Having climbed to try to find its ceiling and being unable to do so, he decided that he would have to hedge-hop all the way back to base. The hazards were trees, telegraph poles and, of course, buildings if his course took him over inhabited areas. Rudel did not know precisely where he was but he decided to fly westward to the limit of his fuel; then if the fog still persisted he would have to make a forced landing. He wanted to put this off for as long as possible so as to be sure he was in friendly territory and not in some remote region dominated by partisans.

In the event the fog did not clear and with visibility limited to a few meters he put his Stuka down in a plowed field. When he switched off the engine he could hear traffic moving; clearly there was a road nearby, and the rear-gunner was sent to investigate. On his return the latter reported that they were in German-occupied territory, that the vehicles they had heard were German trucks and that he now knew precisely where they were. Rudel, anxious to get back to his airfield, was not prepared to wait until the fog lifted. Taxying the Stuka down to the road he turned toward home and 'drove' the aircraft up the road until, nearing the airfield his progress was halted at a railroad grade crossing which was too narrow for the plane to pass. So he completed his journey in an army truck, and that afternoon – in another Stuka – he was flying again.

On Christmas Day 1941 Rudel clocked up his 500th sortie and six days later General Freiherr von Richthofen decorated him with the Deutsches Kreuz in gold. A short spell of leave was followed by a posting to the advanced flying-training school at Graz. Rudel did not want to leave his squadron at the front, but he was sent to Graz to give new Ju87 air crews the benefit of his experience. In the event when he was not lecturing or flying he spent every spare minute on his favorite sports – throwing the discus and the javelin and putting the shot. Rudel was a great physical fitness addict and the fact that he kept in such magnificent condition enabled him to survive a terrible ordeal two years later.

In June 1942 the authorities acceded to Rudel's repeated demands for a posting back to his old Wing at the front and he reported back as the great battle for Stalingrad opened. Somewhere *en route* he contracted jaundice, but he was not prepared to spend very long in hospital. 'In this game,' he said, 'one can't afford to be too long out of action in case you miss some new enemy tactic or plane, perhaps. . . .' By November

Stolze Zahlen von den Einsätzen des Major Rudel.

am 24.7.41 100. Feindflug	vernicht. Panzer:	Auszeichnungen:
" 24.9.42 500. "	mit Bordwaffen 223	
" 10.2.43 1000. "	" Bomben 78	EK II : 10.11.1939
" 1.6.44 2000. "	versenkte Schiffe:	EK I : 18.7.1941
Flugkilometer: 530.000 km	1 Schlachtschiff	Dtsch. Kreuz: 24.4.1942
abgew. Bomben: 1.000.000 kg	1 gr. Kreuzer	Ritterkreuz: 15.1.1942
versch. Munition:	70 Übersetzboote	
1000.000 Schuss MG.	Brennstoff: 5.000.000 L	Eichenlaub: 14.4.1943
150.000 " 2 cm	vernichtete LKw's:	Schwerter: 25.11.1943
5.000 " 3.7 "	600-700 LKw's und	Brillanten: 29.3.194
vernichtet 40-45 Pakstellung.	bespannte Fahrzeuge	
" 45-50 Arie- "	abgesch. Flugzeuge:	
" 35 Flak- "	2 Lagg 3/1 JL-2	

Above: **The greatest exponent of the Ju87 was without doubt Hans-Ulrich Rudel, whose score board lists every achievement, victory, and decoration.**
Left: **The *Gruppenkommandeur* of I/StG2 celebrates his return from his 1000th sortie on 6 April 1944 in the customary fashion. Hauptmann Bauer (with the cup) was awarded the Knight's Cross to the Iron Cross with oakleaves on 18 October 1944.**
Below left: **Hitler presenting Rudel with the *Ritterkreuz.***

1942 he had gained command of the 1st squadron of the 1st Wing of StG2 and was still flying an incredible number of sorties every day. At one time his Stukas were operating from an airfield 40km west of Stalingrad against a Soviet armored division which had broken through the German lines and almost reached the edge of the airfield. German reinforcements were rushed up to seal off the gap and Rudel's Stukas provided support – bombing up and taking off to strike at Soviet tanks less than a kilometer from the end of the airfield. The inadequacy of bombs against tanks was becoming increasingly obvious to the *Stukagruppen*.

On 10 February 1943 Rudel chalked up his 1000th sortie, and his name was now a byword to the German public. He was posted to a special air 'commando' unit formed at Briansk to test the newly developed tank-busting Ju87s. In effect the first live targets for the 37mm cannon of these modified Ju87Ds were Soviet landing craft in the Black Sea, and Rudel is credited with sinking seventy of them in the space of three weeks. In June during a tank battle around Bielgorod he knocked out his first tank with one of the new tank-busters, and nearly knocked himself out at the same time. 'I was inexperienced' he wrote later, 'and I was flying very low, approaching the tank from the rear in a shallow dive. I pressed the firing button when I was about thirty meters away. I got in a short burst, there was a frightful explosion and as I levelled out I found we were flying into a great fireball. I am surprised we came through it unscathed – so too was my rear gunner who said that the tank exploded like a bomb and he had seen bits of it crashing down behind us.'

During Operation Citadel – an assault against the Russian salient west of Kursk – the German advance ground to a halt when it came up against a huge concentration of Soviet armor. German and Soviet tanks slogged away at each other, separated by a no mans land 1200–1800m wide. The Panzer commanders called for Stukas, and Rudel's Wing was quickly on the scene. It was largely because of the brilliant success of the new tank-busters in this action that the *Panzerstaffels* were formed. By this time Rudel had developed a technique for employing them. It was best, he found, to shoot a tank either in the back or the side. The engine of the Soviet T-34 was at the back and the cooling system did not permit thick armor, furthermore the armor-plating was pierced to allow the heat to dissipate and so it was a specially vulnerable area. Attacking the back of the tank thus usually implied flying in from the rear. This had an added advantage for if the plane was hit in the course of the attack the pilot would be flying toward friendly territory and not toward the enemy.

In March 1944 Rudel flew his 1500th operational sortie, was promoted to major, and commanded the third Wing of StG2. Flying was restricted by the weather in the first half of March. Winter was over and the snow and ice had melted, and the roads and airstrips had been churned into the glutinous mud known to the Russians as *Rasputiza*, making movement difficult. In the air, fog and mist made flying equally difficult. Even the birds were walking, Rudel commented. Toward the end of the month the weather started to clear and the tempo of Stuka operations picked up. Rudel's Wing was called upon to destroy a bridge across the Dniestr River at Yainpol in the Ukraine. For once it was a beautifully clear day and because Russian fighters were becoming increasingly troublesome, arrangements had been made for a Wing of German fighters to escort Rudel's planes over the target area. The escort was supposed to rendezvous with the Stukas about 50km from Yainpol. In the event the German fighters were nowhere to be seen when the Stukas reached the rendezvous. However, there was no sign of Soviet fighters so Rudel decided to press on with his mission. Yet he was uneasy because the air crews flying with him in 1944 were not as experienced as their predecessors of 1941 and 1942. Shortage of fuel in Germany and the need to train pilots quickly to replace the heavy casualties sustained by Stuka crews had necessitated cutting back flying time under instruction.

Twenty kilometers from Yainpol the Stukas ran into trouble, when a squadron of Lavochkin La-5 fighters pounced on them. Keeping formation was all important, but some of the German pilots attempted to take evasive action and Rudel swore at them over the radio, 'Keep in formation, and keep together, damn you! I'm frightened as well!'

Then a second hazard appeared. As the Stukas swung into line for their attack, with Rudel in the van, they came under heavy anti-aircraft fire. Rudel released his bomb and saw it strike the ground on the right of the bridge; a strong wind had blown it off course. 'Keep left, left, left,' he radioed to the others as he turned to strafe the Russian anti-aircraft defenses. Meantime two of the Soviet fighters had managed to slip into the line of Stukas and were hot on the tail of one of Rudel's less experienced pilots. The latter panicked, tried to twist and turn away and then headed north into enemy territory. 'Turn, turn!' Rudel yelled into his microphone. However by this time Rudel himself was being chased by a couple of La-5s and before he could do anything about the Stuka which was flying for Kiev he had to extricate himself.

It took fifteen minutes to shake off the Soviet fighters and muster his squadrons into formation. Ordering one of the squadron leaders to take over and see the formation back to base Rudel now turned back. Flying low over the river he succeeded in getting back to the target area without attracting the enemy's notice. The Russian fighters would certainly never expect a lone Stuka to return when the mission had been completed. Rudel continued to fly on in the direction taken by his lost plane; suddenly he saw it. It had crash landed in a field and although the plane was damaged the two man crew seemed to be all right, for they were standing by their Stuka, waving. The ground looked firm, so Rudel – against his better judgment – decided to risk landing.

As soon as he touched the ground the stranded crew raced across, Rudel's rear-gunner slid back the canopy over his cockpit and they climbed in with him. Rudel gunned the engine and tried to take off, but the machine refused to move. One wheel had sunk in the mud, and although the three men climbed down and tried to ease the wheel out of the Russian *rasputiza* they could not release it.

A few minutes later the Germans saw a crowd of Russians bearing down on them from the edge of the field, 400m away. 'Run,' shouted Rudel, jumping down from the plane. The party, with Rudel leading, belted across the field with the Russians in pursuit. Rudel ran in a southerly direction for he had observed that the River Dniestr, which they would have to cross to get to friendly territory, was about six kilometers

Below: **Rudel receiving well-deserved public acclaim after completing 2000 sorties.**

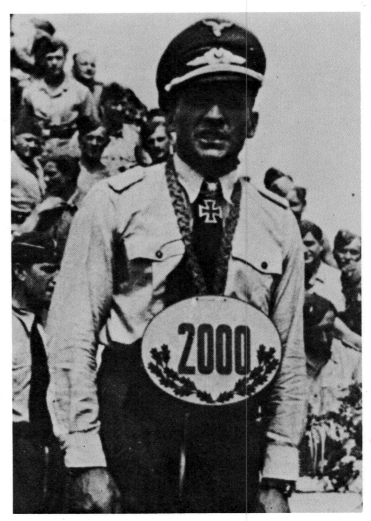

away to the south. Clearly physical fitness would be an asset and fortunately all the four Germans were fit. Covering the distance to the riverbank in record time and outstripping their pursuers they were horrified when they got there, for they found that the bank was more like a cliff, thirty to forty meters high and the steep descent to the black icy water was covered in vicious thorn bushes. They could not afford to waste time if they were to avoid capture, so all four swung themselves down through the bushes – arriving at the river's edge with torn and bleeding hands. Fortunately the thorn bushes provided some welcome cover and they crouched there until it seemed their Russian pursuers had given up the chase and gone away.

The uninviting prospect of having to swim the river now faced them. The Dniestr at this point was about 600m wide and judging by the blocks of ice that were floating past its temperature could barely have been much above zero centigrade. Rudel stripped down to his vest and trousers, stuffing the map, compass and pistol he was carrying into his trouser pocket together with his prized *Ritterkreuz*. The others followed suit and, having reluctantly discarded their boots, plunged into the icy water.

Swimming the Dniestr would have been a tremendous feat at any time. Under these conditions it was little short of a miracle that any of them survived, but three did. The other – Rudel's rear-gunner – drowned only a few meters from the far bank. Rudel plunged back into the river and tried to find the lost man, but it was useless. Exhausted, cold, wet and miserable the three survivors lay on the river bank, until Rudel decided the sooner they moved the better. He wanted to get as far away as possible from the Dniestr before nightfall. With stones cutting their feet and their wet clothes frozen to them they trudged on toward the south. Rudel was feeling extremely hungry by this time. The bombing of the bridge had been his eighth mission that day and he had not had time to snatch a meal between sorties.

Around 1500 they saw three figures in the distance – not very clearly, or they might have noticed that the men they took to be Rumanian soldiers and consequently allies of the Germans were in fact wearing uniforms badged with the hammer and sickle. The three strangers were armed and as the Germans approached they unslung their weapons and pointed them at Rudel and his companions. Rudel, realizing he was about to be taken prisoner, promptly ran off and two of the Russians chased him, firing as they ran. One bullet hit Rudel in the shoulder but he charged on and eventually the two Russians gave up. 'My body was aching and I was losing blood, but I've never run a faster 400m than I did that day,' Rudel said later. However the chase was not over. As he slacked his pace he saw more Russians coming toward him from the right, and running across a plowed field he tripped and fell. At this stage he felt he just could not go on, but he was not prepared to give up. Scraping furiously with his torn and bleeding fingers he lay in a furrow and covered himself with clods of frozen soil. Twice the Russians almost stumbled on him when search parties moving in open order crossed the field. As he lay in his burrow, wet and bleeding but boiling with tension, he saw Stukas of his own Wing fly toward where he had landed. It was a comforting thought to know they were looking for him, even though he was unable to disclose his position.

By nightfall the Russians appeared to have called off the search and Rudel set off south again. Stiff, ravenously hungry, thirsty and in considerable pain from his wound and bleeding feet, he plodded along up hill and down dale, through streams and bogs, taking his direction from the stars as his compass was not luminous. That he was going in the right direction was confirmed when he saw the flashes and heard the dull rumble of artillery fire directly ahead. However it was a long way off and by 2100 Rudel felt that he could go no further; he needed rest and a meal. Up to this point he had meticulously avoided roads and habitations; now he looked for a house standing on its own. When he did find one, he staved off the attentions of some yapping dogs, and broke in. He found that it was occupied by an old and miserably poor couple. The old woman gave him a jug of water and a piece of stale and moldy bread. 'Never,' Rudel said, 'have I enjoyed a meal more!'

Rudel had a brief rest and then stumbled on again. He reached the outskirts of Floreshty soon after dawn. The question now was whether Floreshty was occupied by the Russians or by the Rumanians. The problem was resolved when he heard men speaking German as he crept cautiously into the town. They turned out to be two German sentries who were inclined to be equally as cautious as Rudel. 'Who do you reckon you are?' queried one distrustfully when Rudel addressed them in German. In his rags, dirty and bleeding, he could hardly have been a prepossessing spectacle and Rudel had considerable difficulty convincing them that he was a German officer. It was the production of his *Ritterkreuz* that clinched it. Rudel was taken to a regimental aid post where he was given sandwiches and had his wound dressed. Wrapped in a blanket he was taken by truck to the nearest airstrip at Beltsy. By the time he got there a Ju52 was waiting to transport him back to his own base, where he found that the whole Wing had turned out to cheer him in and a newly baked cake awaited him in the officers' mess.

Rudel owed his freedom to his resourcefulness, his toughness, his optimism and his courage. These qualities were recognized in the citation which led to him being decorated with the '*Ritterkreuz* with Swords and Diamonds' – the highest German decoration for bravery – at the end of March. However Rudel quickly resumed his old routine, still flying his beloved but now obsolete Ju87s and concentrating on tank-busting missions. By the end of the war he had been credited with knocking out a total of 519 Soviet tanks. He had been shot down six times and had escaped unscathed. His luck, as he himself admitted, was indescribable. However, in November 1944 while flying on a mission near Budapest he was shot in the thigh. Within a few days he was back in the cockpit, flying with his leg in a plaster cast. Three months later he was wounded more seriously and for a time it seemed as if his days as a pilot were over. Flying through an Allied anti-aircraft barrage near Lebus, Rudel's right thigh was shattered. He succeeded in bringing the plane down behind the German lines and he was rushed to a field hospital where the leg was amputated. At a hospital in Berlin he had an artificial limb fitted, and he went back to his squadron. When Germany finally capitulated, Rudel was in Bohemia and made his last flight in a Ju87. He had no intention of falling into Communist hands and he flew to the American zone.

As a footnote to this story of a remarkable man, a brief summary of what happened to him in the postwar world seems apt. Following his surrender to the United States troops at Kitzingen where he put down his Stuka, Rudel was interrogated first in Britain and later in France before being taken back to Germany to convalesce in a hospital in Bavaria. When he was discharged from the hospital in 1946 he started work as a haulage contractor. Two years later he emigrated to Argentina where he found a job with the State Airplane Works. However after a few years he returned to Germany, where he continues to pursue his sporting activities with all the enthusiasm he displayed as a Stuka pilot.

APPENDICES

1. The Stuka and *Schlachtflieger* Groups and Wings

This appendix lists the Stuka formations and briefly summarizes their history.

Sturzkampfgeschwader 1 (StG1)

This Group was constituted on 18 November 1939. During the invasion of France and the Low Countries it formed part of the VIII *Fliegerkorps*. In February 1941 it was transferred from France to Sicily to serve under command of the X *Fliegerkorps* and participated in attacks on the British Mediterranean Fleet and Malta. April 1941 saw the Group back with the VIII *Fliegerkorps* for the Balkans campaign and in May it supported the airborne invasion of Crete. In June 1941 it was transferred to the Eastern Front for the assault on the USSR.

On 18 October 1943 the group was redesignated *Schlachtgeschwader 1*(SG1). In March 1941 the group began to convert from Ju87s to Focke-Wulf 190s. It was disbanded on 8 May 1945.

Wing 1 (IStG1)

Officially, the first Wing of the group was not posted to it until 17 June 1943. Prior to that it had been known as the IV(Stuka) Training Group I *Lehrgeschwader*. As part of the group its designation was changed on 18 October 1943 to ISG1. During its existence this Wing served on the northern and central sectors of the Russian front.

Wing 2 (IIStG1)

Raised originally in Wertheim, this Wing was designated IIIStG5 in May 1939 becoming IIStG1 on 9 July 1940 after service in Poland. In January 1941 it was transferred to the Mediterranean area, participating in attacks on Malta and the Balkan campaigns. In June 1941 it was transferred back to Germany for Operation Barbarossa. Between April and June 1944 the Wing converted to FW190s and it was disbanded in Flensburg on 8 May 1945.

Wing 3 (IIIStG1)

In October 1939 the 4th(Stuka) 186 T squadron was formed for service with the aircraft carrier *Graf Zeppelin* then under construction. In September 1939 the squadron was expanded to become the *Trägersturzkampfgruppe* I/186 which on 9 July 1940 was redesignated IIIStG1. (Subsequently on 18 October 1943 it became IIISG1.)

The original naval squadron, 4th(St)186 T, took part in the Polish campaign and the whole Wing fought in the Battle of Britain. In February 1941 IIIStG1 was deployed in Sicily for anti shipping operations in the Mediterranean and in April and May it flew sorties in support of the campaign in North Africa. Based in Greece, the Wing participated in the battle of Crete and was then transferred to the Russian front. In March 1944 it converted to FW190s and, like the two other Wings of StG1, was disbanded on 8 May 1945.

Sturzkampfgeschwader 2 Immelmann (StG2)
Schlachtgeschwader 2 Immelmann (SG2)

This was the Luftwaffe's first dive-bomber formation. As a Stuka Wing, known then as *Fliegergruppe Schwerin* it was raised in 1934. The traditional sobriquet, Immelmann, was bestowed on it on 3 April 1935 and the Wing was raised to Group status in May 1939. On 18 October 1943 it was redesignated *Schlachtgeschwader 2* and as such fought through to the end of the war. Some of the Luftwaffe's most famous Stuka aces, including Oberst Dinort, Oberst Dr Ernst Kupfer and Rudel commanded this Group at one time or another.

Wing 1 (IStG2)

Originally a squadron formed in Cottbus in May 1939, IStG2 participated in every campaign of World War II. Starting with Poland it was continually on active service – in the Battle of Britain, the Balkans, the assault on Crete and on the Eastern Front. On 18 October 1943 (when the *Störkampfstaffel* [harassment squadrons] were organized into *Nachtschlachtgruppen* [Night Harassment Wings]) IStG2 was redesignated ISG2. In the summer of 1944 it was finally converted to FW190s. At the end of the war the Wing was in Austria where it was disbanded.

Wing 2 (IIStG2)

When the StG2 Group was formed in May 1939 an existing Wing I162 was redesignated IIStG2 and allotted to it. However for most of its service this Wing was detached from the Group and functioned as an independent formation. On 12 January 1942 IIStG2 was redesignated IIIStG3 and a new Wing was allotted to the Group. When the latter became a *Schlachtgeschwader* the original IIStG2 was under the command of the 4th Air Fleet (*Luftflotte* 4). It continued to fly Ju87s on dive-bombing missions until March 1944 when two of the Wings squadrons were turned into independent tank destroyer squadrons – the 10(Pz)SG3 and 77.

Meanwhile the new Wing which in October 1943 was renamed IISG2 joined the Group on the Eastern Front where it served until the end of the war.

Wing 3 (IIIStG2)

Raised originally in May 1939 this Wing participated in the Polish campaign, the Battle of Britain, the Balkan campaigns and the assault on Crete. From 22 June 1941 until the end of the war – when it was in Czechoslovakia – it operated on the Russian Front, and was one of the few Stuka formations to fly Ju87s to the bitter end. It was disbanded near Prague in May 1945.

Sturzkampfgeschwader 3 (StG3)
Schlachtgeschwader 3 (SG3)

This Group was formed in June and July 1940 at Dinard in France, the headquarters staff being transferred from the 28th Bomber Group (KG28). For a long time, however, its Wings functioned as independent units and the Group exercised little control over them. The first Wing assigned to the Group was originally IStG76, known colloquially as the *Graz-er Gruppe* because it was stationed in Graz (Austria) when StG3 was constituted. Similarly the second Wing, stationed in Insterburg in East Prussia, and known within the Group as the 'Insterburg Wing' did not come under command until January 1942 when the Wing was designated IStG3. The third

Wing was that which was originally – on paper – the second Wing of StG2 Immelmann (IIStG2) was redesignated IIIStG3 on 13 January 1942. Finally when the Stuka Groups became *Schlachtgeschwader* on 18 October 1943 all three Wings were redesignated I, II and IIISG3.

StG3 and later SG3 was the one Stuka Group which operated with its Wings widely dispersed. However between February 1941 and April 1943 it operated in support of Rommel's Afrika Korps and became known by the sobriquet *Afrika Geschwader*. At the beginning of 1944 it was moved to the Russian Front where it operated on the northern and central sectors until the end of hostilities.

Wing 1 (IStG3)

Raised originally in Lübeck-Blankensee, this Wing moved in May 1939 to Graz, where it was redesignated IStG76, becoming IStG3 on 9 July 1940. In common with the other Stuka units it was redesignated ISG3 on 18 October 1943. In July 1944 the Wing converted to FW 190s.

As IStG76 the unit was deployed in Poland and France and subsequently, as IStG3, fought in the Battle of Britain, the Balkan campaigns, the assault on Crete and in North Africa. From February to July 1943 it was engaged in operations in the southern sector of the Russian Front. It had another spell of duty back in the Mediterranean area, before being transferred back to the northern sector of the Russian Front.

Wing 2 (IIStG3)

Formed at Insterburg this Wing was designated IStG2 in May 1939. It was incorporated in StG3 as the Group's second Wing in January 1942, when it was redesignated IIStG3. As such it spent the remainder of the war on the Russian Front.

Wing 3 (IIIStG3)

Raised in Jever/Oldenburg in July 1939 it was designated IIStG2 in May 1939, redesignated IIIStG3 in January 1942 and finally IIISG3 on 18 October 1943. As IIStG2 it took part in the campaigns in Poland and France, and in the Battle of Britain. In January 1941 the Wing moved to Sicily where it was engaged on antishipping operations and subsequently in support of the Afrika Korps. Like the other two Wings of the Group, IIISG3 was operating on the Russian Front when the war ended.

The Panzerjägerstaffel (Tank Destroyer Squadron)

In March 1944 a tank-busting squadron, originally formed under the auspices of the 2nd Stuka Group and known as 4StG2, was redesignated 10(Pz)SG3. It was transferred to SG3 under whose command it spent the rest of the war.

Sturzkampfgeschwader 77 (StG77)
Schlachtgeschwader 77 (SG77)

The StG77 was the first Stuka Group to function as such when it was deployed with headquarters and two Wings in Poland. When, in common with the other *Sturzkampfgeschwader* it was redesignated a *Schlachtgeschwader* (SG77) the first SG1 Wing (ISG1) was transferred to SG77 to become the Group's second Wing (IISG77). At the same time the Group's original second Wing (IISG77) was cross-posted to SG10 and was redesignated IIISG10.

Another change effected about that time was the incorporation of a Tank Destroyer squadron from StG1 into the Group. This squadron was designated 10(Pz)SG77. Its stay with this group was shortlived because it was transferred shortly afterward to SG3 to become 10(Pz)SG3. In turn it was replaced by 6(Pz)SG2.

This Group is recorded as having flown over 30,000 sorties between September 1939 and 15 July 1942. By May 1944 its record stood at 100,000 sorties. Its three Wings gave up their Stukas and converted to FW190s in July 1944. From June 1941 it was employed entirely on the Russian Front.

Wing 1 (IStG77)

Formed originally in Kitzingen, Bavaria, it was designated IStG51 at the beginning of May 1939 and redesignated IStG77 two weeks later.

Wing 2 (IIStG77)

Raised in Schweinfurt, Lower Franconia, in 1937 the Wing was designated IIStG77 in May 1939. Five years later it was transferred as IISG77 to SG10 as the third Wing (IIISG10). In its place ISG1 was redesignated IISG77.

Wing 3 (IIIStG77)

Following the campaign in France in 1940 the third Wing of StG88 was raised by converting squadrons of the Luftwaffe's 2nd Bomber Group (IIKG76). It was redesignated IIISG77 in October 1943.

IV (Stuka) Lehrgeschwader 1 (IStG5)
(The Stuka Training Group)

'Training Group I,' which was raised in Neubrandenburg and Greifswald during 1934 and 1935, was the Luftwaffe's original Bomber Group. The fourth Wing of this Group developed the techniques of dive bombing and undertook the training of the dive bombers. After the campaign in Poland this Wing, then known as IV(Stuka)LG1, was detached from Training Group 1 to become an independent Stuka Wing. In January 1942 it was redesignated IStG5.

The Wing saw service in Poland and France and participated in the Battle of Britain before it was sent to the northern sector of the Russian Front in 1942. It was based in Finland and was employed mainly on antishipping operations on the Barents Sea, harassing convoys carrying supplies to Murmansk.

In June 1943 the IStG5 became the first Wing of StGl and was redesignated IStG1 and was under command of this Group for the rest of the war. However when IStG5 became IStG1 a new IStG5 was raised in Norway and allocated to *Luftflotte* 5. 4StG5 formed the nucleus of this Wing, which was redesignated ISG5 in October 1943 when the Stuka Groups all became *Schlachtgeschwader*. In 1944 the Wing converted to FW190s but continued to operate in the northern sector of the Eastern Front. However in January 1945 the Wing was redesignated yet again, becoming IIIKG200, and was transferred to the Western Front where most of its missions were directed against targets in the Netherlands. It was disbanded on 8 May 1945 in Schleswig-Holstein.

2. Performance Data

Specifications of the Ju87A-I

Span	45ft 3.5in
Length	35ft 5.5in
Height	12ft 9.5in
Wing Area	343,368sq ft
Weight Empty	5104lb
Loaded	7495lb
Armament	One fixed forward-firing 7.92mm MG17 machine gun and one 7.92mm MG15 machine gun on flexible mounting in rear cockpit. Bomb load; one 250kg (550lb) or, flown as a single seater, one 500kg (1100lb) bomb
Powerplant	One 12-cylinder liquid-cooled Junkers Jumo 210 Ca engine rated at 600hp for takeoff
Speeds Maximum	200mph at 12,000ft
Cruising	171mph at 8860ft
Service ceiling	23,000ft
Range Maximum	620 miles at 162mph
Type	Two-seater dive bomber and ground attack aircraft

Specifications of the Ju87B-1

Span	45ft 3.5in
Length	36ft 5in
Height	13ft 2in
Wing Area	343,368sq ft
Weight Empty	about 6080lb
Maximum loaded	9371lb
Armament	Two fixed forward-firing 7.92mm MG17 machine guns and one 7.92mm MG15 machine gun on flexible mounting in the rear cockpit. Bomb load; one 500kg (1100lb) or one 250kg (550lb) and four 50kg (110lb) bombs
Powerplant	One 1200hp 12-cylinder inverted-vee liquid-cooled Junkers Jumo 211 Da engine
Speed Maximum	242mph
Service ceiling	26,250ft
Range	With maximum bomb load 373 miles
Type	Two-seater dive bomber

Specifications of the Ju87D-1

Span	45ft 3.5in
Length	37ft 8.75in
Height	12ft 9.5in
Wing Area	343sq ft
Weight Empty	8598lb
Normally loaded	12,600lb
Maximum loaded	14,565lb
Armament	Two fixed forward-firing 7.92mm MG17 machine guns and one 7.92mm twin machine gun on a flexible mounting in the rear cockpit. Bomb load; one 1800kg (3968lb) for short-range delivery, or one 1000kg (2200lb), or two 500kg (1100lb) or four 250kg bombs in the main bomb rack below the fuselage, *plus* four 50kg or two 100kg bombs in the wing racks. (Alternatively two pods containing up to six machine guns or two 20mm cannon, or two containers containing approximately 100 2kg antipersonel grenades could be carried.)
Powerplant	One 12-cylinder liquid-cooled Junkers Jumo 211J-1 engine rated at 1400hp for takeoff and 1410hp at an altitude of 4500m
Speeds Maximum	With normal load 255mph at 13,500ft
Normal cruising	198mph at 16,500ft
Range Maximum	954 miles at 16,500ft
	Time to reach altitude of 16,500ft 20 minutes
Service ceiling	With maximum load 15,500ft; with normal (12,600lb) load 24,000ft
Type	Two-seater dive bomber and close-support aircraft

Right: A formation of Ju87D-3s operating on the Eastern front. The undersurfaces of the wing tips and fuselage bands were the yellow tactical markings used in this theater of operations.

3. Production of Close-support Combat Aircraft during World War II

Model	1939	1940	1941	1942	1943	1944	1945	Total
Ju87	134	603	500	960	1072	1012	—	4281
Hs129			7	221	411	202	—	841
FW190				68	1183	4279	1104	6634
Ju88						3	—	3
	134	603	507	1249	2666	5496	1104	11,759

In 1935-36 about 265 Hs123 planes were produced.

4. Glossary of German Air Force Terms and Abbreviations

A/B Schule: Flying Training School (Single-engined aircraft)
A-Stand: Forward gunner's position
Aufklärung: Reconnaissance
Befehlshaber: Commander
Beobachter: Observer
Besatzung: Air Crew
BK: Bordkanone (fixed aircraft cannon)
Bodenpersonal: ground staff
Bordfunker: wireless operator
Bordschütze: air gunner
Bola: Bodenlafette (ventral gun mounting)
Buna: Trade name for a synthetic rubber used for tires, fuel, tanks etc
C-Amt: Technical Department of the Technisches Amt of the RLM
C-Stand: Ventral gunner's position
DB: Daimler-Benz
DLH: Deutsche Lufthansa (German State Airline)
Einsatzkommando: Operational Detachment
EKdo: Erprobungs-Kommando (Proving or Test Detachment)
Erprobungs-: Proving- or Test-
Entwicklungs-: Development-
Ergänzungs-: Replacement
Erprobungsstelle: Proving (or Test) Center (Abbrev: E-Stelle)
Ersatz: Replacement or Substitute
Feldwebel: Equivalent to Sergeant (RAF) or Airman 1st Class (USAF)
Fernaufklärung: Long-range reconnaissance
Fernnachtjagd: Long-range night interception or intrusion
FFS: Flugzeugführerschule: Pilot's School
Flächenziel: area target
Flak: Fliegerabwehrkanone: anti-aircraft gun
Flugzeugführer: Pilot
FuG: Funkgerät: radio or radar set
Führungsstab: Operations Staff
FZG: Fernzielgerät: Remote aiming device/bomb sight
Gefreiter: Leading Aircraftsman (RAF) or Airman 3rd Class (USAF)
General der Jagdflieger: General of Fighters
General der Kampfflieger: General of Bombers
General der Nachtjagd: General of Night Fighting
Geschwader: Group
Gruppe: Equivalent to Wing (RAF)
Gruppenkommandeur: Officer commanding a Gruppe
Hauptmann: Equivalent to Flight Lieutenant (RAF) or Captain (USAF)
Heeres-: Army-
Jabo: Jagdbomber: Fighter bomber
Jabo-Rei: Jagdbomber mit vergrösserter Reichweite: Extended-range fighter-bomber
Jagd-: Fighter-, chase, pursuit
JG: Jagdgeschwader: Fighter Group
JGr: Jagdgruppe: Fighter Wing
Jumo: Junkers Motorenbau
Kampf-: Battle
Kampfgeschwader: Bomber Group (Battle Group)

Kampfzerstörer: Heavy Fighter (Battle Destroyer)
Kdo: Kommando: Detachment
Kette: Element of three aircraft
KG: Kampfgeschwader: Bomber Group
Langstrecken-: Long-range-
Luftwaffenführungsstab: Luftwaffe Operations Staff
Luftwaffengeneralstab: Luftwaffe Air Staff
Major: Equivalent to Squadron Leader (RAF) or Major (USAF)
MK: Maschinenkanone: Machine cannon
NJG: Nachtjagdgeschwader: Night-Fighter Group
NSGr: Nachtschlachtgruppe: Night-Harassment Wing
ObdL Oberbefehlshaber der Luftwaffe: Commander in Chief of the Luftwaffe
Oberleutnant: Equivalent of Flying Officer (RAF) or First Lieutenant (USAF)
OKH: Oberkommando des Heeres: Army High Command
OKL: Oberkommand der Luftwaffe: Luftwaffe High Command
Projekt: Project
PaK: Panzerabwehrkanone: Anti-tank cannon
Panzerstaffel: Tank (Destroyer) Squadron
Panzerbombe: Armor-piercing bomb
Punktziel: Precision target
Pz: Panzer: Tank or Armor
Reichs-: State-
Ritterkreuz: Knight's Cross of the Iron Cross. First of five grades of the highest German decoration for bravery, the higher grades being signified by the addition of Oak Leaves, Oak Leaves and Swords, Diamonds, Golden Oak Leaves, Diamonds and Swords.
RLM: Reichsluftfahrtministerium: State Ministry of Aviation
Rotte: A pair of aircraft (usually fighters) flying in loose formation
SC: Splitterbombe: Fragmentation bomb
Sch G.: Schlachtgeschwader: Close-support or Assault group
Schlacht: Close support or assault
Schlachtgeschwader: Close-support or Assault Group
Schwarm: section of four fighters
SG: Sondergerät: Special Equipment
Sonder: Special
Stab: Staff
Stabsschwarm: Staff section (in a Gruppe)
Staffel: equivalent to Squadron (RAF)
Staffelkapitän: Squadron commander (regardless of rank)
St G: Sturzkampfgeschwader or Stukageschwader: Dive-Bomber Group
Störkampfstaffel: Night-Harassment Squadron
Stuka: Abbreviation of Sturzkampfflugzeug: Dive Bomber
Sturm: Assault (for example, Sturmgruppe: Assault Wing)
Stuvi: Sturz(kampf)visier: Dive-bombing sight
Technisches Amt: Technical Office of the RLM
Versuchs-: Experimental-
Verband, Verbände: Formation, formations
VS: Verstell(luft)schraube: Variable-pitch airscrew
Waffenprüfplatz: Weapons Proving Ground
Wüstennotstaffel: Desert (or Wilderness) Rescue Squadron
ZG: Zerstörungsgeschwader: Destroyer or Heavy-Fighter Group

Bibliography

The Warplanes of the Third Reich, William Green
Stuka-Oberst Hans-Ulrich Rudel, Günther Just
Trotzdem, Hans-Ulrich Rudel
Stuka, Peter C Smith
Stukas! Erlebnisse eines Fliegerkorps, Curt Strohmeyer
Das waren die deutschen Jagdflieger Asse 1939–1945,
   R F Toliver/T J Constable

Acknowledgments

The author would like to thank the following individuals and agencies for supplying the photographs and artworks:

Aeronautical and Military Photographs, Berlin: pp 20–21.

Aeronautica Militaire: pp 20 (top left), 26–27 (bottom), 31 (bottom), 32 (top), 35 (center right), 44–45 (bottom), 46 (top), 46–47 (bottom and top left).
Bison Picture Library: pp 2–3, 7, 9 (top), 10 (top), 11 (top), 13 (top right), 14 (bottom), 16, 19, 23 (top right), 25, 26 (top right), 28 (bottom), 29 (bottom), 33 (top left and right), 36 (bottom and top), 41 (center and bottom), 42 (top both), 43 (all three), 48, 57 (bottom) 58, 62.
Bryan Philpott via R L Ward: pp 7 (bottom).

8–9 (bottom), 34–35, 37 (top), 44 (top right), 48, 49 (top right, center and bottom), 51 (top both and bottom), 57 (top and center).
Bundesarchiv: pp 1, 4–5, 12–13 (bottom), 13 (top left), 18, 22–23 (bottom), 22 (top left), 24, 27 (top left), 28–29 (bottom), 30 (top), 32–33 (bottom), 34–35 (center), 41 (center right), 42 (center), 45 (top and center left), 47 (top), 50, 51 (second from bottom), 54, 55.
Gordon Bain: pp 38–39.
Imperial War Museum: p 31 (center).

Messerschmitt: pp 10–11 (bottom).
Taylor Picture Library: pp 14–15 (center), 31.
USAF: p 64.
National Archives: p 8 (top).

Artwork:

Mike Badrocke: cutaway on pp 40–41, line drawings on p 43.
Mike Bailey: Cover sideview.
Mike Trim: Sideview on p 42.

Below: The name 'Jocelyn' was probably added to this Ju87D at the same time as the underwing USAAF markings. The slipstream driven diving sirens have been removed from the wheel spats, and there are no wing mounted machine guns. The underwing dive brakes are not fitted, this being an omission which started with the D-5 as the dive-bombing role gradually gave way to a normal ground attack/support role. The top of the pilot's seat was 10mm armor plate and the back 8mm.